"Jack Canfield and Mark Victor Hansen have done it again. Another superb helping of *Chicken Soup for the Soul!*"

Rick Dees
Weekly Top 40

"There is no such thing as too much *Chicken Soup for the Soul.* The powerful stories in *A 4th Course* will make you keep coming back for more and more servings of love, hope and inspiration."

Rudy Ruettiger

"Uplift yourself, your soul and your spirit. *A 4th Course of Chicken Soup for the Soul* will fill you with love, joy, warmth and good feelings about yourself, your future and other people."

Lou Tice
international educator, lecturer and author,
Personal Coaching for Results: How to Mentor and Inspire Others to Amazing Growth

"*A 4th Course of Chicken Soup for the Soul* is simple, inspiring and a must-read for anyone. A must-read for everyone."

Fran A. Tarkenton

"*A 4th Course of Chicken Soup for the Soul* is the perfect mirror of the love, wisdom and inspiration within all of us. Read it and remember!"

Cathy Lee Crosby
author, *Let the Magic Begin*

"About *A 4th Course* . . . As usual, Jack and Mark have captured the essence of love and understanding between human beings. Having just lost my dad and missing him, oh, so dearly, "On Parenting" brought back many, many smiles that Dad and I shared together. I just thank my lucky stars that each time we met or parted, Dad and I would hug and kiss each other with warmth, pride and joy."

producer, *Am*

"My heart and soul are touched again by the magic of *Chicken Soup for the Soul*. These heart-touching, soul-penetrating stories have stimulated me to new possibility thinking. *A 4th Course of Chicken Soup* is the best book yet!"

Dr. Robert H. Schuller

"The stories in *A 4th Course of Chicken Soup for the Soul* brought warmth to me and reassurance that there are still some decent, caring and compassionate human beings in the world."

Lloyd Bridges

"I have been hungry for this fourth serving of *Chicken Soup*. We need to be reminded that life is a magnificent, compassionate, enthralling adventure (with occasional thunderstorms), and this remarkable menu of reminders fills the bill (la fare) perfectly. Bon appétit!"

Peter McWilliams
author, *DO IT!, LIFE 101, You Can't Afford the Luxury of a Negative Thought, LOVE 101, How to Grow Yourself*

"More love, more encouragement and more incredible insights into living life on higher ground! I can't wait for the next *Soup* serving!"

Glenna Salsbury
professional speaker and author, *The Art of the Fresh Start*

A 4th Course of

CHICKEN SOUP
FOR THE SOUL®

A 4th Course of Chicken Soup for the Soul
More Stories to Open the Heart and Rekindle the Spirit
Jack Canfield, Mark Victor Hansen, Hanoch McCarty, Meladee McCarty

Published by Backlist, LLC,
a unit of Chicken Soup for the Soul Publishing, LLC. www.chickensoup.com

Front cover redesign by Andrea Perrine Brower
Originally published in 1997 by Health Communications, Inc.

Back cover and spine redesign by Pneuma Books, LLC

Distributed to the booktrade by Simon & Schuster. SAN: 200-2442

Publisher's Cataloging-in-Publication Data
(Prepared by The Donohue Group)

A 4th course of chicken soup for the soul : more stories to open the
heart and rekindle the spirit / [compiled by] Jack Canfield ... [et
al.].

   p. : ill. ; cm.

   Originally published: Deerfield Beach, FL : Health Communications, c1997.
   ISBN: 978-1-62361-044-9

1. Spiritual life--Anecdotes. 2. Anecdotes. I. Canfield, Jack, 1944- II. Title:
Fourth course of chicken soup for the soul

BL624 .A14 2012
158.1/28   2012913032

PRINTED IN THE UNITED STATES OF AMERICA
on acid free paper

22 21 20 19 18 17 16 15 14 13   01 02 03 04 05 06 07 08 09 10

A 4th Course of
CHICKEN SOUP FOR THE SOUL®

More Stories to Open the Heart and Rekindle the Spirit

Jack Canfield
Mark Victor Hansen
Hanoch McCarty
Meladee McCarty

CSS

Backlist, LLC, a unit of
Chicken Soup for the Soul Publishing, LLC
Cos Cob, CT
www.chickensoup.com

Contents

3. ON PARENTS AND PARENTING

4. ON TEACHING AND LEARNING

5. ON DEATH AND DYING

6. A MATTER OF PERSPECTIVE

7. OVERCOMING OBSTACLES

8. ECLECTIC WISDOM

Introduction

In days past, people sat around the kitchen table and talked. Laughter was shared between husband and wife, and wisdom was passed from grandparent to child. The stories that were told were the glue that bonded hearts and held families and friends together.

With all that humans have gained with technology, computers and television, we have lost something special to humanity. It is time to once again share our stories, heart to heart.

Patty Hansen

Everyone has a story. No matter what we do for a living, how much we have in our bank account or what the color of our skin is, we have a story. Each one of us has a story, whether it is visible to the eye or it is locked inside of us. We are encouraged to believe that our past, our circumstances, both physical and emotional, and our experiences are our story. Our mental picture of our life's story encompasses what we perceive to be true about ourselves and our possibilities.

The life one is born into is not necessarily our destiny. All of us have the power to rewrite our story, to recast the drama of our lives and to redirect the actions of the main character, ourselves. The outcomes of our lives are determined mainly by our responses to each event. Do we choose to be hero or victim in our lives' dramas?

Good stories, like the best mentors in our lives, are *door openers*. They are unique experiences containing insights tied to emotional triggers that get our attention and stay in our memories. These stories can free us from being bound to decisions of the past and open us to understanding ourselves and the opportunities that are there before us. A really good story allows us to recognize the choices that are open to us and see new alternatives we might never have seen before. It can give us permission to try (or at least consider trying) a new path.

Many of the people you will meet in these pages provide a model to follow of unconditional acts of kindness and love, of great courage and foresight, of belief when cynicism would be the norm, a sense of hope in what the world has to offer, and the inspiration to seek it for ourselves.

Some of the stories you will refer to again and again because the message is one of comfort and encouragement. Other stories will inspire you to share them with your family, friends and colleagues.

How to Read This Book

We have had the tremendous opportunity to receive feedback from readers all over the world. Some have shared with us that they get the most value if they read our books from cover to cover. Others focus in depth on a particular chapter that interests them. Most people tell us that they find it works best to read one or two stories at a time, and really savor the feelings and lessons that the stories evoke. Our advice is to take your time and really let each story effect you at a deep level. Ask yourself how you could apply the lessons learned to your own life. Engage each story as if it mattered, as if it could make a real difference in your life.

Compiling these stories has taken a lot of work. We hope you will love these stories as we have loved them. May they bring you tears, laughter, insight, healing and empowerment.

We hope that we can in a small way contribute to your life by bringing you these models of ordinary people doing extraordinary things to guide you on your journey. We wish for you that, in the pages of this book there is a story that holds the key to doors that need opening in your life.

Jack Canfield, Mark Victor Hansen,
Hanoch McCarty and Meladee McCarty

From a Previous Reader

Dear Sirs:

I am writing you from a military base in Panama to thank you for your marvelous book and to share with you the impact it has had on my life and upon those with whom I have shared it.

I was alone in my hotel room one night after working extended hours when I read the story "Information Please" in *A 3rd Serving of Chicken Soup for the Soul.* I am not ashamed to confess that I cried profusely and found something healing in those tears. At that point I wrote a poem for you which I have enclosed.

Later I shared your book with a Marine who was in charge of guarding access to classified information. He was the third in line of armed security making his job the least demanding and the most boring. Because of this his superior officer had given him permission to read, but he had forgotten a book. It was going to be a long 12-hour watch for him so I gave him a copy of *A 3rd Serving of Chicken Soup for the Soul,* which I had in my briefcase. I warned him, however, that he might be caught in the act of "unMarine-like" emotional catharsis after reading some of the stories.

I entered the hallway at the end of our watch and found another armed Marine standing next to the first.

Both of them had moist eyes as one said, "Kinda gets you, doesn't it?"

The other Marine replied, "Roger that," and walked off. Seeing me, he said, "Thanks for the book, Lieutenant. I'm going to the exchange first thing tomorrow to buy me one."

"Told you there were some zingers in there," I said, and we bid each other good night.

Thanks for a great book. I recommend it to everybody. Here's the poem.

Tell me a story, my heart is empty.
Let the tears flow, my eyes are dry.
Too long has discouragement bound me.
Lift my soul, let me fly.

Tell me a story, my hope has diminished.
Tell me of faith and love.
Remind me that we are created
To live on earth as in heaven above.

Tell me a story, fill my heart with compassion.
Open my eyes, I've been blind.
Remind me that all men are brothers,
That we all should be loving and kind.

Serve me another helping,
More Chicken Soup for My Soul.
To love let us encourage each other,
That higher dimensions of love may we know.

Lieutenant Morris Passmore, USNR

1

ON LOVE

A chemist who can extract from his heart's element, compassion, respect, longing, patience, regret, surprise, and forgiveness and compound them into one can create that atom which is called love.

Kahlil Gibran

A Friend on the Line

Life without a friend is death without a witness.

Spanish Proverb

Even before I finished dialing, I somehow knew I'd made a mistake. The phone rang once, twice—then someone picked it up.

"You got the wrong number!" a husky male voice snapped before the line went dead. Mystified, I dialed again.

"I said you got the wrong number!" came the voice. Once more the phone clicked in my ear.

How could he possibly know I had a wrong number? At that time, I worked for the New York City Police Department. A cop is trained to be curious—and concerned. So I dialed a third time.

"Hey, c'mon," the man said. "Is this you again?"

"Yeah, it's me," I answered. "I was wondering how you knew I had the wrong number before I even said anything."

"You figure it out!" The phone slammed down.

I sat there awhile, the receiver hanging loosely in my

fingers. I called the man back.

"Did you figure it out yet?" he asked.

"The only thing I can think of is . . . nobody ever calls you."

"You got it!" The phone went dead for the fourth time. Chuckling, I dialed the man back.

"What do you want now?" he asked.

"I thought I'd call . . . just to say hello."

"Hello? Why?"

"Well, if nobody ever calls you, I thought maybe I should."

"Okay. Hello. Who is this?"

At last I had gotten through. Now *he* was curious. I told him who I was and asked who he was.

"My name's Adolf Meth. I'm 88 years old, and I haven't had this many wrong numbers in one day in 20 years!" We both laughed.

We talked for 10 minutes. Adolf had no family, no friends. Everyone he had been close to had died. Then we discovered we had something in common: he'd worked for the New York City Police Department for nearly 40 years. Telling me about his days there as an elevator operator, he seemed interesting, even friendly. I asked if I could call him again.

"Why would you wanta do that?" he asked, surprised.

"Well, maybe we could be phone friends. You know, like pen pals."

He hesitated. "I wouldn't mind . . . having a friend again." His voice sounded a little tentative.

I called Adolf the following afternoon and several days after that. Easy to talk with, he related his memories of World Wars I and II, the Hindenburg disaster and other historic events. He was fascinating. I gave him my home and office numbers so he could call me. He did—almost every day.

I was not just being kind to a lonely old man. Talking with Adolf was important to me, because I, too, had a big gap in my life. Raised in orphanages and foster homes, I never had a father. Gradually, Adolf took on a kind of fatherly importance to me. I talked about my job and college courses, which I attended at night.

Adolf warmed to the role of counselor. While discussing a disagreement I'd had with a supervisor, I told my new friend, "I think I ought to have it out with him."

"What's the rush?" Adolf cautioned. "Let things cool down. When you get as old as I am, you find out that time takes care of a lot. If things get worse, *then* you can talk to him."

There was a long silence. "You know," he said softly, "I'm talking to you just the way I'd talk to a boy of my own. I always wanted a family—and children. You're too young to know how that feels."

No, I wasn't. I'd always wanted a family—and a father. But I didn't say anything, afraid I wouldn't be able to hold back the hurt I'd felt for so long.

One evening Adolf mentioned his 89th birthday was coming up. After buying a piece of fiberboard, I designed a 2' x 5' greeting card with a cake and 89 candles on it. I asked all the cops in my office and even the police commissioner to sign it. I gathered nearly a hundred signatures. Adolf would get a kick out of this, I knew.

We'd been talking on the phone for four months now, and I thought this would be a good time to meet face to face. So I decided to deliver the card by hand.

I didn't tell Adolf I was coming; I just drove to his address one morning and parked the car up the street from his apartment house.

A postman was sorting mail in the hallway when I entered the building. He nodded as I checked the mailboxes for Adolf's name. There it was. Apartment 1H, some 20 feet from where I stood.

My heart pounded with excitement. Would we have the same chemistry in person that we had on the phone? I felt the first stab of doubt. Maybe he would reject me the way my father rejected me when he went out of my life. I tapped on Adolf's door. When there was no answer, I knocked harder.

The postman looked up from his sorting. "No one's there," he said.

"Yeah," I said, feeling a little foolish. "If he answers his door the way he answers his phone, this may take all day."

"You a relative or something?"

"No. Just a friend."

"I'm really sorry," he said quietly, "but Mr. Meth died day before yesterday."

Died? Adolf? For a moment, I couldn't answer. I stood there in shock and disbelief. Then, pulling myself together, I thanked the postman and stepped into the late-morning sun. I walked toward the car, misty-eyed.

Then, rounding a corner, I saw a church, and a line from the Old Testament leaped to mind: A friend loveth at all times. And especially in death, I realized. This brought a moment of recognition. Often it takes some sudden and sad turn of events to awaken us to the beauty of a special presence in our lives. Now, for the first time, I sensed how very close Adolf and I had become. It had been easy, and I knew this would make it even easier the next time, with my next close friend.

Slowly, I felt a warmth surging through me. I heard Adolf's growly voice shouting, "Wrong number!" Then I heard him asking why I wanted to call again.

"Because you mattered, Adolf," I said aloud to no one. "Because I was your friend."

I placed the unopened birthday card on the back seat of my car and got behind the wheel. Before starting the engine, I looked over my shoulder. "Adolf," I whispered, "I didn't get the wrong number at all. I got you."

Jennings Michael Burch

Simple Wooden Boxes

It is the heart that makes a man rich. He is rich according to what he is, not according to what he has.

Henry Ward Beecher

I suppose everyone has one particular childhood Christmas that stands out more than any other. For me, it was the year that the Burlington factory in Scottsboro closed down. I was only a small child. I could not name for you the precise year; it is an insignificant blur in my mind, but the events of that Christmas will live forever in my heart.

My father, who had been employed at Burlington, never let on to us that we were having financial difficulties. After all, children live in a naive world in which money and jobs are nothing more than jabberwocky, and for us the excitement of Christmas could never be squelched. We knew only that our daddy, who usually worked long, difficult hours, was now home more than we had ever remembered; each day seemed to be a holiday.

Mama, a homemaker, now sought work in the local textile mills, but jobs were scarce. Time after time, she was told no openings were available before Christmas, and it was on the way home from one such distressing interview that she wrecked our only car. Daddy's meager unemployment check would now be our family's only source of income. For my parents, the Christmas season brought mounds of worries, crowds of sighs and tears and cascades of prayers.

I can only imagine what transpired between my parents in those moments when the answer came. Perhaps it took a while for the ideas to fully form. Perhaps it was a merging of ideas from both of my parents. I don't know for sure how the idea took life, but somehow it did. They would scrape together enough money to buy each of us a Barbie doll. For the rest of our presents, they would rely on their talents, using scraps of materials they already had.

While dark, calloused hands sawed, hammered and painted, nimble fingers fed dress after dress after dress into the sewing machine. Barbie-sized bridal gowns, evening gowns . . . miniature clothes for every imaginable occasion pushed forward from the rattling old machine. Where we were while all of this was taking place, I have no idea. But somehow my parents found time to pour themselves into our gifts, and the excitement of Christmas was once again born for the entire family.

That Christmas Eve, the sun was just setting over the distant horizon when I heard the roar of an unexpected motor in the driveway. Looking outside, I could hardly believe my eyes. Uncle Buck and Aunt Charlene, Mama's sister and her husband, had driven all the way from Georgia to surprise us. Packed tightly in their car, as though no air were needed, sat my three cousins, my "Aunt" Dean, who refused to be called "Aunt," and both my grandparents. I also couldn't help but notice innumerable gifts for all of us, all neatly packaged and tied with beautiful bows. They had known that it would be a difficult Christmas and they had come to help.

The next morning we awoke to more gifts than I ever could have imagined. And, though I don't have one specific memory of what any of the toys were, I know that there were mountains of toys. Toys! Toys! Toys!

And it was there, amidst all that jubilation, that Daddy decided not to give us his gifts. With all of the toys we had gotten, there was no reason to give us the dollhouses that he had made. They were rustic and simple red boxes, after all. Certainly not as good as the store-bought gifts that Mama's family had brought. The music of laughter filled the morning, and we never suspected that, hidden somewhere, we each had another gift.

When Mama asked Daddy about the gifts, he confided his feelings, but she insisted he give us our gifts. And so, late that afternoon, after all of the guests had gone, Daddy reluctantly brought his gifts of love to the living room.

Wooden boxes. Wooden boxes, painted red, with hinged lids, so that each could be opened and used as a house. On either side was a compartment just big enough to store a Barbie doll, and all the way across, a rack on which to hang our Barbie clothes. On the outside was a handle, so that when it was closed, held by a magnet that looked remarkably like an equal sign, the house could be carried suitcase style. And, though I don't really remember any of the other gifts I got that day, those boxes are indelibly etched into my mind. I remember the texture of the wood, the exact shade of red paint, the way the pull of the magnet felt when I closed the lid, the time-darkened handles and hinges . . . I remember how the clothes hung delicately on the hangers inside, and how I had to be careful not to pull Barbie's hair when I closed

the lid. I remember everything that is possibly remem-
berable, because we kept and cherished those boxes long
after our Barbie doll days were over.

I have lived and loved 29 Christmases, each new and
fresh with an air of excitement all its own. Each filled with
love and hope. Each bringing gifts, cherished and longed
for. But few of those gifts compare with those simple,
wooden boxes. So it is no wonder that I get teary-eyed
when I think of my father, standing there on that cold
Christmas morning, wondering if his gift was good enough.

Love, Daddy, is always good enough.

Martha Pendergrass Templeton

A Family for Freddie

I remember the first time I saw Freddie. He was standing in his playpen at the adoption agency where I work. He gave me a toothy grin. *What a beautiful baby,* I thought.

His boarding mother gathered him into her arms. "Will you be able to find a family for Freddie?"

Then I saw it. Freddie had been born without arms.

"He's so smart. He's only 10 months old, and already he walks and talks." She kissed him. "Say 'book' for Mrs. Blair."

Freddie grinned at me and hid his head on his boarding mother's shoulder. "Now, Freddie, don't act that way," she said. "He's really very friendly," she added. "Such a good, good boy."

Freddie reminded me of my own son when he was that age, the same thick dark curls, the same brown eyes.

"You won't forget him, Mrs. Blair? You will try?"

"I won't forget."

I went upstairs and got out my latest copy of the Hard-to-Place list.

Freddie is a 10-month-old white Protestant boy of English and French background. He has brown eyes, dark-brown hair and fair skin. Freddie was born without arms, but is otherwise in good health. His boarding mother feels he is of superior mentality, and he is already walking and saying a few words. Freddie is a warm, affectionate child who has been surrendered by his natural mother and is ready for adoption.

He's ready, I thought. *But who is ready for him?*

It was 10 o'clock on a lovely late-summer morning, and the agency was full of couples—couples having interviews, couples meeting babies, families being born. These couples nearly always have the same dream: They want a child as much like themselves as possible, as young as possible, and most important—a child with no problems.

"If he develops a problem after we get him," they say, "that is a risk we'll take just like any other parents. But to pick a baby who already has a problem, that's too much."

And who can blame them?

I wasn't alone in looking for parents for Freddie. Any of the caseworkers meeting a new couple started with a hope: maybe they were for Freddie. But summer slipped into fall, and Freddie was with us for his first birthday.

"Freddie is so-o-o big," said Freddie, laughing. "So-o-o big."

And then I found them.

It started out as it always does—an impersonal record in my box, a new case, a new Home Study, two people who wanted a child. They were Frances and Edwin Pearson. She was 41. He was 45. She was a housewife. He was a truck driver.

I went to see them. They lived in a tiny white frame house, in a big yard full of sun and old trees. They greeted me together at the door, eager and scared to death.

Mrs. Pearson produced steaming coffee and oven-warm cookies. They sat before me on the sofa, close together, holding hands. After a moment, Mrs. Pearson began. "Today is our wedding anniversary. Eighteen years."

"Good years." Mr. Pearson looked at his wife. "Except—"

"Yes," she said. "Except. Always the 'except.'" She looked around the room. "It's too neat," she said. "You know?"

I thought of my own living room with my three children. Teenagers now. "Yes," I said. "I know."

"Perhaps we're too old?"

I smiled. "You don't think so," I said. "We don't either."

"You always think it will be this month, and then next month," Mr. Pearson said. "Examinations. Tests. All kinds of things. Over and over. But nothing ever happened. You just go on hoping and hoping, and time keeps slipping by."

"We've tried to adopt before this," Mr. Pearson said. "One agency told us our apartment was too small, so we got this house. Then another agency said I didn't make enough money. We had decided that was it, but this friend told us about you, and we decided to make one last try."

"I'm glad," I said.

Mrs. Pearson glanced at her husband proudly. "Can we choose at all?" she asked. "A boy for my husband?"

"We'll try for a boy," I said. "What kind of boy?"

Mrs. Pearson laughed. "How many kinds are there? Just a boy. My husband is very athletic. He played football in high school; basketball, too, and track. He would be good for a boy."

Mr. Pearson looked at me. "I know you can't tell exactly," he said, "but can you give us any idea how soon? We've waited so long."

I hesitated. There is always this question.

"Next summer maybe," said Mrs. Pearson. "We could take him to the beach."

"That long?" Mr. Pearson said. "Don't you have anyone at all. There must be a little boy somewhere." After a pause he went on, "Of course, we can't give him as much as other people. We haven't a lot of money saved up."

"We've got a lot of love," his wife said. "We've saved up a lot of that."

"Well," I said cautiously, "there is a little boy. He is 13 months old."

"Oh," Mrs. Pearson said, "just a beautiful age."

"I have a picture of him," I said, reaching for my purse. I handed them Freddie's picture. "He is a wonderful little boy," I said. "But he was born without arms."

They studied the picture in silence. He looked at her. "What do you think, Fran?"

"Kickball," Mrs. Pearson said. "You could teach him kickball."

"Athletics are not so important," Mr. Pearson said. "He can learn to use his head. Arms he can do without. A head, never. He can go to college. We'll save for it."

"A boy is a boy," Mrs. Pearson insisted. "He needs to play. You can teach him."

"I'll teach him. Arms aren't everything. Maybe we can get him some."

They had forgotten me. But maybe Mr. Pearson was right, I thought. Maybe sometime Freddie could be fitted with artificial arms. He did have nubs where arms should be.

"Then you might like to see him?"

They looked up. "When could we have him?"

"You think you might want him?"

Mrs. Pearson looked at me. "Might?" she said. "Might?"

"We want him," her husband said.

Mrs. Pearson went back to the picture. "You've been waiting for us," she said. "Haven't you?"

"His name is Freddie," I said, "but you can change it."

"No," said Mr. Pearson. "Frederick Pearson—it's good together."

And that was it.

There were formalities, of course; and by the time we set the day, Christmas lights were strung across city streets and wreaths were hung everywhere.

I met the Pearsons in the waiting room. There was a little snow on them both.

"Your son's here already," I told them. "Let's go upstairs and I'll bring him to you."

"I've got butterflies," Mrs. Pearson announced. "Suppose he doesn't like *us*?'"

I put my hand on her arm. "I'll get him," I said.

Freddie's boarding mother had dressed him in a new white suit, with a sprig of green holly and red berries embroidered on the collar. His hair shone, a mop of dark curls.

"Going home," Freddie said to me, smiling, as his boarding mother put him in my arms.

"I told him that," she said. "I told him he was going to his new home."

She kissed him, and her eyes were wet.

"Good-bye, dear. Be a good boy."

"Good boy," said Freddie cheerfully. "Going home."

I carried him upstairs to the little room where the Pearsons were waiting. When I got there, I put him on his feet and opened the door.

"Merry Christmas," I said.

Freddie stood uncertainly, rocking a little, gazing intently at the two people before him. They drank him in.

Mr. Pearson knelt on one knee. "Freddie, come here. Come to Daddy."

Freddie looked back at me for a moment. Then, turning, he walked slowly toward them, and they reached out their arms and gathered him in.

Abbie Blair

"Today is my teacher's birthday, and for her present I'm staying home."

A Birthday Song

Three things in human life are important: The first is to be kind. The second is to be kind. And the third is to be kind.

Henry James

One morning, John Evans shuffled into my life. A ragged-looking boy, he was decked out in oversized hand-me-down clothes and worn-out shoes that split apart at the seams.

John was the son of black migrant workers who had recently arrived in our small North Carolina town for a season of apple picking. These laborers were the poorest of the poor, earning barely enough to feed their families.

Standing at the head of our second-grade class that morning, John Evans was a hapless sight. He shifted from foot to foot as our teacher, Mrs. Parmele, penned his name in the roll book. We weren't sure what to make of the shoddy newcomer, but whispers of disapproval began drifting from row to row.

"What is that?" the boy behind me mumbled. "Somebody open a window," a girl said, giggling. Mrs.

Parmele looked up at us from behind her reading glasses. The murmuring stopped, and she went back to her paperwork.

"Class, this is John Evans," Mrs. Parmele announced, trying to sound enthusiastic. John looked around and smiled, hoping somebody would smile back. Nobody did. He kept on grinning anyway.

I held my breath, hoping Mrs. Parmele wouldn't notice the empty desk next to mine. She did and pointed him in that direction. He looked over at me as he slid into the seat, but I averted my eyes so he wouldn't think that I had promise as a new friend.

By the end of his first week, John had found firm footing at the bottom of our school's social ladder. "It's his own fault," I told my mother one evening at dinner. "He barely even knows how to count."

My mother had grown to know John quite well through my nightly commentary. She always listened patiently but rarely uttered more than a pensive "Hmmm" or "I see."

"Can I sit by you?" John stood in front of me, lunch tray in hand and a grin on his face. I looked around to see who was watching.

"Okay," I replied feebly.

As I watched him eat and listened to him ramble on, it dawned on me that maybe some of the ridicule heaped on John was unwarranted. He was actually pleasant to be around and was by far the most chipper boy I knew.

After lunch, we joined forces to conquer the play-ground, moving from monkey bars to swingset to sand-box. As we lined up behind Mrs. Parmele for the march back to class, I made up my mind that John would remain friendless no longer.

"Why do you think the kids treat John so badly?" I asked one night as Mother tucked me into bed.

"I don't know," she said sadly. "Maybe that's all they know."

"Mom, tomorrow is his birthday; and he's not going to get anything. No cake. No presents. Nothing. Nobody even cares."

Mother and I both knew that whenever a kid had a birthday, his mother would bring cupcakes and party favors for the entire class. Between my birthday and my sister's, my mom had made several trips herself over the years. But John's mother worked all day in the orchards. His special day would go unnoticed.

"Don't worry," Mom said as she kissed me good night. "I'm sure everything will turn out fine." For the first time in my life, I thought she might be wrong.

At breakfast the next morning, I announced that I wasn't feeling well and wished to stay home.

"Does this have anything to do with John's birthday?" Mother asked. The bright-red flush on my cheeks was the only answer she needed. "How would you like it if your only friend didn't show up on your birthday?" she asked gently. I thought it over for a moment and then kissed her good-bye.

I wished John a happy birthday first thing in the morning; and his embarrassed smile showed me that he was glad I had remembered. Maybe it wouldn't be such a horrible day after all.

By mid-afternoon I had almost decided that birthdays weren't that big a deal. Then, as Mrs. Parmele was writing math equations on the blackboard, I heard a familiar sound coming from the hallway. A voice I knew was singing the birthday song.

Moments later, Mother came through the door with a tray of cupcakes aglow with candles. Tucked under her arm was a smartly wrapped present with a red bow on top.

Mrs. Parmele's high-pitched voice joined in while the

class stared at me for an explanation. Mother found John looking like a deer caught in car headlights. She put the cupcakes and gift on his desk and said, "Happy birthday, John."

My friend graciously shared his cupcakes with the class, patiently taking the tray from desk to desk. I caught Mother watching me. She smiled and winked as I bit into moist chocolate frosting.

Looking back, I can scarcely remember the names of the children who shared that birthday. John Evans moved on shortly thereafter, and I never heard from him again. But whenever I hear that familiar song, I remember the day its notes rang most true: in the soft tones of my mother's voice, the glint in a boy's eyes and the taste of the sweetest cupcake.

Robert Tate Miller

When Kevin Won

Maturity begins to grow when you can sense your concern for others outweighing your concern for yourself.

John MacNoughton

If you had to choose one word to describe Kevin, it might have been "slow." He didn't learn his ABCs as fast as other kids. He never came in first in the schoolyard races. However, Kevin had a special rapport with people. His smile was brighter than the sun in June; his heart bigger than the mountain sky. Kevin's enthusiasm for life was quite contagious, so when he discovered that the pastor at his church, Randy, was putting together a boys' basketball team, his mother could only answer, "Yes, you may join."

Basketball became the center of Kevin's life. At practice, he worked so hard you'd have thought he was preparing for the NBA. He liked to stand in a certain spot near the free-throw line and shoot baskets. Patiently, he stood there throwing ball after ball after ball, until finally it would swish through the hoop. "Look at me, Coach!" he'd yell at Randy, jumping up and down, his face just glowing with the thrill of it all.

The day before their first game, Coach Randy gave each player a bright red jersey. Kevin's eyes absolutely turned to stars when he saw his—number 12. He scrambled himself into the sleeves and scarcely ever took it off again. One Sunday morning, the sermon was interrupted by Kevin's excited voice. "Look, Coach!" He lifted his gray wool sweater to reveal his beautiful red jersey to God and everyone.

Kevin and his whole team truly loved basketball. But just loving the game doesn't help you win. More balls fell out of the basket than into it, and the boys lost every game that season by very large margins, except one . . . the night it snowed and the other team couldn't make it to the game.

At the end of the season, the boys played in the church league's tournament. As the last-place team, they drew the unfortunate spot of playing against the first-place team— the tall, undefeated first-place team. The game went pretty much as expected, and near the middle of the fourth quarter Kevin's team stood nearly 30 points behind.

At that point, one of Kevin's teammates called time-out. As he came to the side, Randy couldn't imagine why the time-out had been called. "Coach," said the boy. "This is our last game and I know that Kevin has played in every game, but he's never made a basket. I think we should let Kevin make a basket." With the game completely out of reach, the idea seemed reasonable, so plans were made. Every time Kevin's team had the ball, Kevin was to stand in his special spot near the free-throw line and they would give him the ball. Kevin skipped extra high as he went back onto the court.

His first shot bounced around but missed. Number 17 from the other team swiped the ball and took it down to the other end scoring two more points. As soon as Kevin's team had the ball again, they passed it to Kevin who obediently stood in his place. But he missed again. This pattern continued a few more times until Number 17 grew wise. He grabbed one of the rebounds and instead of running off down the court, he threw the ball to Kevin who shot . . . and missed again.

Soon, all the players were circling Kevin, throwing the ball to him and clapping for him. It took the spectators just a little longer to figure out what was happening, but little by little people started to stand up and clap their hands. The whole gymnasium thundered with the clapping, hollering, chanting, "Kevin! Kevin!" And Kevin just kept shooting.

Coach Randy realized the game must be over. He looked up at the clock which was frozen with 46 seconds left. The referees stood by the scoring table, cheering and clapping like everyone else. The whole world was stopped, waiting and wanting for Kevin.

Finally, after an infinite amount of tries, the ball took one miraculous bounce and went in. Kevin's arms shot high into the air and he shouted, "I won! I won!" The clock ticked off the last few seconds and the first-place team remained undefeated. But on that evening, everyone left the game truly feeling like a winner.

Janice M. Gibson
as told to her by Rev. Steve Goodier

A Mason-Dixon Memory

Dondre Green glanced uneasily at the civic leaders and sports figures filling the hotel ballroom in Cleveland. They had come from across the nation to attend a fund-raiser for the National Minority College Golf Scholarship Foundation. I was the banquet's featured entertainer. Dondre, an 18-year-old high school senior from Monroe, Louisiana, was the evening's honored guest.

"Nervous?" I asked the handsome young man in his starched white shirt and rented tuxedo.

"A little," he whispered, grinning.

One month earlier, Dondre had been just one more black student attending a predominantly white Southern school. Although most of his friends and classmates were white, Dondre's race was never an issue. Then, on April 17, 1991, Dondre's black skin provoked an incident that made nationwide news.

"Ladies and gentlemen," the emcee said, "our special guest, Dondre Green."

As the audience stood applauding, Dondre walked to the microphone and began his story. "I love golf," he said quietly. "For the past two years, I've been a member of the

St. Frederick High School golf team. And though I was the
only black member, I've always felt at home playing at
mostly white country clubs across Louisiana."

The audience leaned forward; even the waiters and
busboys stopped to listen. As I listened, a memory buried
in my heart since childhood fought its way to life.

"Our team had driven from Monroe," Dondre continued. "When we arrived at the Caldwell Parish Country
Club in Columbia, we walked to the putting green."

Dondre and his teammates were too absorbed to notice
the conversation between a man and St. Frederick athletic
director James Murphy. After disappearing into the club-
house, Murphy returned to his players.

"I want to see the seniors," he said. "On the double!" His
face seemed strained as he gathered the four students,
including Dondre.

"I don't know how to tell you this," he said, "but the
Caldwell Parish Country Club is reserved for whites
only." Murphy paused and looked at Dondre. His teammates glanced at each other in disbelief.

"I want you seniors to decide what our response should
be," Murphy continued. "If we leave, we forfeit this tournament. If we stay, Dondre can't play."

As I listened, my own childhood memory from 32 years
ago broke free.

In 1959, I was 13 years old, a poor black kid living with my
mother and stepfather in a small black ghetto on Long Island,
New York. My mother worked nights in a hospital, and my
stepfather drove a coal truck. Needless to say, our standard
of living was somewhat short of the American dream.

Nevertheless, when my eighth-grade teacher
announced a graduation trip to Washington, D.C., it never
crossed my mind that I would be left behind. Besides a
complete tour of the nation's capital, we would visit Glen
Echo Amusement Park in Maryland. In my imagination,

Glen Echo was Disneyland, Knott's Berry Farm and Magic Mountain rolled into one.

My heart beating wildly, I raced home to deliver the mimeographed letter describing the journey. But when my mother saw how much the trip cost, she just shook her head. We couldn't afford it.

After feeling sad for 10 seconds, I decided to try to fund the trip myself. For the next eight weeks, I sold candy bars door-to-door, delivered newspapers and mowed lawns. Three days before the deadline, I'd made just barely enough. I was going!

The day of the trip, trembling with excitement, I climbed onto the train. I was the only nonwhite in our section.

Our hotel was not far from the White House. My roommate was Frank Miller, the son of a businessman. Leaning together out of our window and dropping water balloons on tourists quickly cemented our new friendship.

Every morning, almost a hundred of us loaded noisily onto our bus for another adventure. We sang our school fight song dozens of times, en route to Arlington National Cemetery and even on an afternoon cruise down the Potomac River.

We visited the Lincoln Memorial twice, once in daylight, the second time at dusk. My classmates and I fell silent as we walked in the shadows of those 36 marble columns, one for every state in the Union that Lincoln labored to preserve. I stood next to Frank at the base of the 19-foot seated statue. Spotlights made the white Georgian marble glow. Together, we read those famous words from Lincoln's speech at Gettysburg remembering the most bloody battle in the War between the States: "... we here highly resolve that these dead shall not have died in vain—that this nation, under God shall have a new birth of freedom ..."

As Frank motioned me into place to take my picture, I took one last look at Lincoln's face. He seemed alive and so terribly sad.

The next morning, I understood a little better why he wasn't smiling. "Clifton," a chaperone said, "could I see you for a moment?"

The other guys at my table, especially Frank, turned pale. We had been joking about the previous night's direct water-balloon hit on a fat lady and her poodle. It was a stupid, dangerous act, but luckily nobody got hurt. We were celebrating our escape from punishment when the chaperone asked to see me.

"Clifton," she began, "do you know about the Mason-Dixon line?"

"No," I said, wondering what this had to do with drenching fat ladies.

"Before the Civil War," she explained, "the Mason-Dixon line was originally the boundary between Maryland and Pennsylvania—the dividing line between the slave and free states." Having escaped one disaster, I could feel another brewing. I noticed that her eyes were damp and her hands were shaking.

"Today," she continued, "the Mason-Dixon line is a kind of invisible border between the North and the South. When you cross that invisible line out of Washington, D.C., into Maryland, things change."

There was an ominous drift to this conversation, but I wasn't following it. Why did she look and sound so nervous?

"Glen Echo Amusement Park is in Maryland," she said at last, "and the management doesn't allow Negroes inside." She stared at me in silence.

I was still grinning and nodding when the meaning finally sank in.

"You mean I can't go to the park," I stuttered, "because I'm a Negro?"

She nodded slowly. "I'm sorry, Clifton," she said, taking my hand.

"You'll have to stay in the hotel tonight. Why don't you and I watch a movie on television?"

I walked to the elevators feeling confusion, disbelief, anger and a deep sadness. "What happened, Clifton?" Frank said when I got back to the room. "Did the fat lady tell on us?"

Without saying a word, I walked over to my bed, lay down and cried. Frank was stunned into silence. Junior-high boys didn't cry, at least not in front of each other.

It wasn't just missing the class adventure that made me feel so sad.

For the first time in my life, I learned what it felt like to be a "nigger."

Of course there was discrimination in the North, but the color of my skin had never officially kept me out of a coffee shop, a church—or an amusement park.

"Clifton," Frank whispered, "what is the matter?"

"They won't let me go to Glen Echo Park tonight," I sobbed.

"Because of the water balloon?" he asked.

"No," I answered, "because I'm a Negro."

"Well, that's a relief!" Frank said, and then he laughed, obviously relieved to have escaped punishment for our caper with the balloons. "I thought it was serious."

Wiping away the tears with my sleeve, I stared at him. "It is serious. They don't let Negroes into the park. I can't go with you!" I shouted. "That's pretty damn serious to me."

I was about to wipe the silly grin off Frank's face with a blow to his jaw when I heard him say, "Then I won't go either."

For an instant we just froze. Then Frank grinned. I will never forget that moment. Frank was just a kid. He wanted to go to that amusement park as much as I did, but there was something even more important than the class night out. Still, he didn't explain or expand.

The next thing I knew, the room was filled with kids listening to Frank. "They don't allow Negroes in the park,"
he said, "so I'm staying with Clifton."

"Me, too," a second boy said.

"Those jerks, " a third muttered. "I'm with you, Clifton."
My heart raced. Suddenly, I was not alone. A pint-sized
revolution had been born. The "water-balloon brigade," 11
white boys from Long Island, had made its decision: "We
won't go." And as I sat on my bed in the center of it all, I
felt grateful. But, above all, I was filled with pride.

Dondre Green's story brought that childhood memory
back to life. His golfing teammates, like my childhood
friends, faced an important decision. If they stood by their
friend it would cost them dearly. But when it came time to
decide, no one hesitated. "Let's get out of here," one of
them whispered.

"They just turned and walked toward the van," Dondre
told us. "They didn't debate it. And the younger players
joined us without looking back."

Dondre was astounded by the response of his friends—
and the people of Louisiana. The whole state was out-
raged and tried to make it right. The Louisiana House of
Representatives proclaimed a Dondre Green Day and
passed legislation permitting lawsuits for damages, attor-
neys' fees and court costs against any private facility that
invites a team, then bars any member because of race.

As Dondre concluded, his eyes glistened with tears. "I
love my coach and my teammates for sticking by me," he
said. "It goes to show that there are always good people
who will not give in to bigotry. The kind of love they
showed me that day will conquer hatred every time."

My friends, too, had shown that kind of love. As we sat
in the hotel, a chaperone came in waving an envelope.
"Boys!" he shouted. "I've just bought 13 tickets to the
Senators-Tigers game. Anybody want to go?"

The room erupted in cheers. Not one of us had ever been to a professional baseball game in a real baseball park.

On the way to the stadium, we grew silent as our driver paused before the Lincoln Memorial. For one long moment, I stared through the marble pillars at Mr. Lincoln, bathed in that warm, yellow light. There was still no smile and no sign of hope in his sad and tired eyes.

"... We here highly resolve ... that this nation, under God, shall have a new birth of freedom ... "

In his words and in his life, Lincoln made it clear that freedom is not free. Every time the color of a person's skin keeps him out of an amusement park or off a country-club fairway, the war for freedom begins again. Sometimes the battle is fought with fists and guns, but more often the most effective weapon is a simple act of love and courage.

Whenever I hear those words from Lincoln's speech at Gettysburg, I remember my 11 white friends, and I feel hope once again. I like to imagine that when we paused that night at the foot of his great monument, Mr. Lincoln smiled at last.

Clifton Davis

Beautiful on the Inside

Love is a wonderful thing. You never have to take it away from one person to give it to another. There's always more than enough to go around.

Pamela J. deRoy

Lisa, my two-year-old daughter, and I were walking down the street toward home one sunny morning when two elderly women stopped in front of us. Smiling down at Lisa, one of them said, "Do you know you are a very beautiful little girl?"

Sighing and putting her hand on her hip, Lisa replied in a bored voice, "Yes, I know!"

A bit embarrassed by my daughter's seeming conceit, I apologized to the two ladies and we continued our walk home. All the way there, I was trying to determine how I was going to handle this situation.

After we went into the house, I sat down and stood Lisa in front of me. I gently said, "Lisa, when those two ladies spoke to you, they were talking about how pretty you are on the outside. It's true you are pretty on the outside.

That's how God made you. But a person needs to be beautiful on the inside, too." As she looked at me uncompre-
hendingly, I continued.

"Do you want to know how a person is beautiful on the
inside?" She nodded solemnly.

"Okay. Being beautiful on the inside is a choice you
make, honey, to be good to your parents, a good sister to
your brother and a good friend to the children you play
with. You have to care about other people, honey. You
have to share your toys with your playmates. You need to
be caring and loving when someone is in trouble or gets
hurt and needs a friend. When you do all those things,
you are beautiful on the inside. Do you understand what
I'm saying?"

"Yes, Mommy, I'm sorry I didn't know that," she
replied. Hugging her, I told her I loved her and that I
didn't want her to forget what I'd said. The subject never
came up again.

Nearly two years later, we moved from the city to the
country and enrolled Lisa in a preschool program. In her
class was a little girl named Jeanna, whose mother had
died. The child's father had recently married a woman
who was energetic, warm and spontaneous. It was readily
apparent that she and Jeanna had a wonderful, loving
relationship.

One day Lisa asked if Jeanna could come over to play
for an afternoon, so I made arrangements with her stepmother to take Jeanna home with us the next day after the
morning session.

As we were leaving the parking lot, the following day
Jeanna said, "Can we go see my mommy?"

I knew her stepmother was working, so I said cheerfully, "Sure, do you know how to get there?" Jeanna said
she did and, following her directions, I soon found myself
driving up the gravel road into the cemetery.

My first response was one of alarm as I thought of the possible negative reaction of Jeanna's parents when they learned what had happened. However, it was obvious that visiting her mother's grave was very important to her, something she needed to do; and she was trusting me to take her there. Refusing would send her a message that it was wrong of her to want to go there.

Outwardly calm, as though I'd known this was where we were going all along, I asked, "Jeanna, do you know where your mother's grave is?"

"I know about where it is," she responded.

I parked on the road in the area she indicated and we looked around until I found a grave with her mother's name on a small marker.

The two little girls sat down on one side of the grave and I sat on the other and Jeanna started talking about how things had been at home in the months leading up to her mother's death, as well as what had happened on the day she died. She spoke for some time and all the while Lisa, with tears streaming down her face, had her arms around Jeanna and, patting her gently, said quietly over and over, "Oh, Jeanna, I'm so sorry. I'm so sorry your mother died."

Finally, Jeanna looked at me and said, "You know, I still love my mommy and I love my new mommy, too."

Deep in my heart, I knew that this was the reason she'd asked to come here. Smiling down at her, I said reassuringly, "You know, Jeanna, that's the wonderful thing about love. You never have to take it away from one person to give it to another. There's always more than enough to go around. It's kind of like a giant rubberband that stretches to surround all the people you care about." I continued, "It's perfectly fine and right for you to love both your mothers. I'm sure your own mother is very glad that you have a new mommy to love you and take care of you and your sisters."

Smiling back at me, she appeared satisfied with my response. We sat quietly for a few moments and then we all stood up, brushed ourselves off and went home. The girls played happily after lunch until Jeanna's stepmother came to pick her up.

Briefly, without going into a lot of detail, I told her what had occurred that afternoon and why I'd handled things as I had. To my profound relief, she was very understanding and appreciative.

After they left, I picked Lisa up in my arms, sat down on a kitchen chair, kissed her cheek and hugged her tightly and said, "Lisa, I'm so proud of you. You were such a wonderful friend to Jeanna this afternoon. I know it meant a lot to her that you were so understanding and that you cared so much and felt her sadness."

A pair of lovely, dark brown eyes looked seriously into mine as my daughter added, "Mommy, was I beautiful on the inside?"

Pamela J. deRoy

Such As I Have

What you keep to yourself you lose, what you give away, you keep forever.

Axel Munthe

With only two weeks before Christmas, the last place I wanted to be was in the hospital recovering from surgery. This was our family's first Christmas in Minnesota, and I wanted it to be memorable, but not this way.

For weeks I had ignored the pain in my left side, but when it got worse, I saw the doctor. "Gallstones," he said, peering at the x rays. "Enough to string a necklace. You'll need surgery right away."

Despite my protests that this was a terrible time to be in the hospital, the gnawing pain in my side convinced me to go ahead with surgery. My husband, Buster, assured me he could take care of things at home, and I called a few friends for help with carpooling. A thousand other things—Christmas baking, shopping and decorating—would have to wait.

I struggled to open my eyes after sleeping for the better part of two days in the hospital following my surgery.

As I became more alert, I looked around to what seemed like a Christmas floral shop. Red poinsettias and other bouquets crowded the windowsill. A stack of cards waited to be opened. On the stand next to my bed stood a small tree decorated with ornaments my children had made. The shelf over the sink held a dozen red roses from my parents in Indiana and a yule log with candles from our neighbor. I was overwhelmed by all the love and attention.

Maybe being in the hospital around Christmas isn't so bad after all, I thought. My husband said that friends had brought meals to the family and offered to look after our four children.

Outside my window, heavy snow was transforming our small town into a winter wonderland. The kids have to be loving this, I thought as I imagined them bundled in their snowsuits building a backyard snowman, or skating at Garfield School on the outdoor ice rink.

Would they include Adam, our handicapped son? I wondered. At five years old, he had just started walking independently, and I worried about him getting around on the ice and snow with his thin ankles. Would anyone take him for a sled ride at the school?

"More flowers!" The nurse's voice startled me from my thoughts as she came into the room carrying a beautiful centerpiece. She handed me the card while she made room for the bouquet among the poinsettias on the windowsill.

"I guess we're going to have to send you home," she teased. "We're out of space here!"

"Okay with me," I agreed.

"Oh, I almost forgot these!"

She took more cards from her pocket and put them on the tray. Before leaving the room, she pulled back the pale green privacy curtain between the two beds.

While I was reading my get-well cards, I heard, "Yep, I like those flowers."

I looked up to see the woman in the bed beside me push the curtain aside so she could see better. "Yep, I like your flowers," she repeated.

My roommate was a small 40-something woman with Down's syndrome. She had short, curly, gray hair and brown eyes. Her hospital gown hung untied around her neck, and when she moved forward it exposed her bare back. I wanted to tie it for her, but I was still connected to an IV. She stared at my flowers with childlike wonder.

"I'm Bonnie," I told her. "What's your name?"

"Ginger," she said, rolling her eyes toward the ceiling and pressing her lips together after she spoke. "Doc's gonna fix my foot. I'm gonna have *suur-jeree* tomorrow."

Ginger and I talked until dinnertime. She told me about the group home where she lived and how she wanted to get back for her Christmas party. She never mentioned a family, and I didn't ask. Every few minutes she reminded me of her surgery scheduled for the next morning. "Doc's gonna fix my foot," she would say.

That evening I had several visitors, including my son Adam. Ginger chattered merrily to them, telling each about my pretty flowers. But mostly, she kept an eye on Adam. And, later after everyone left, Ginger repeated over and over, just as she had about my flowers, "Yep, I like your Adam."

The next morning Ginger left for surgery, and the nurse came to help me take a short walk down the hall. It felt good to be on my feet.

Soon I was back in our room. As I walked through the door, the stark contrast between the two sides of the room hit me. Ginger's bed stood neatly made, waiting for her return. But she had no cards, no flowers and no visitors. My side bloomed with flowers, and the stack of get-well cards reminded me of just how much I was loved.

No one sent Ginger flowers or a card. In fact, no one had even called or visited.

Is this what it will be like for Adam one day? I wondered, then quickly put the thought from my mind.

I know, I decided. I'll give her something of mine.

I walked to the window and picked up the red-candled centerpiece with holly sprigs. But this would look great on our Christmas dinner table, I thought, as I set the piece back down. What about the poinsettias? Then I realized how much the deep-red plants would brighten the entry of our turn-of-the-century home. And, of course, I can't give away Mom and Dad's roses, knowing we won't see them for Christmas this year, I thought.

The justifications kept coming: the flowers are beginning to wilt; this friend would be offended; I really could use this when I get home. I couldn't part with anything. Then I climbed back into my bed, placating my guilt with a decision to call the hospital gift shop when it opened in the morning and order Ginger some flowers of her own.

When Ginger returned from surgery, a candy-striper brought her a small green Christmas wreath with a red bow. She hung it on the bare white wall above Ginger's bed. That evening I had more visitors, and even though Ginger was recuperating from surgery, she greeted each one and proudly showed them her Christmas wreath.

After breakfast the next morning, the nurse returned to tell Ginger that she was going home. "The van from the group home is on its way to pick you up," she said.

I knew Ginger's short stay meant she would be home in time for her Christmas party. I was happy for her, but I felt my own personal guilt when I remembered the hospital gift shop would not open for two more hours.

Once more I looked around the room at my flowers. Can I part with any of these?

The nurse brought the wheelchair to Ginger's bedside. Ginger gathered her few personal belongings and pulled her coat from the hanger in the closet.

"I've really enjoyed getting to know you, Ginger," I told her. My words were sincere, but I felt guilty for not following through on my good intentions.

The nurse helped Ginger with her coat and into the wheelchair. Then she removed the small wreath from the nail on the wall and handed it to Ginger. They turned toward the door to leave when Ginger said, "Wait!"

Ginger stood up from her wheelchair and hobbled slowly to my bedside. She reached her right hand forward and gently laid the small wreath in my lap.

"Merry Christmas," she said. "You're a nice lady." Then she gave me a big hug.

"Thank you," I whispered.

I couldn't say anything more as she hobbled back to the chair and headed out the door.

I dropped my moist eyes to the small wreath in my hands. Ginger's only gift, I thought. And she gave it to me.

I looked toward her bed. Once again, her side of the room was bare and empty. But as I heard the "ping" of the elevator doors closing behind Ginger, I knew that she possessed much, much more than I.

Bonnie Shepherd

A Hair-Raising Experience

The test of courage comes when we are in the minority.

Ralph W. Sackman

As an only child to two adoring parents, I grew up believing that life was good. Especially when my mom washed my long black hair. I loved it because I always got great head scratches! But on one particular day, a huge clump of my long hair fell out in my mother's hands, much to her horror. She thought she had done something terribly wrong. Little did we know this was the beginning of a nine-year odyssey.

Over the next six years, I lost large amounts of my hair and was always trying to shield these bald spots from the world. None of the doctors could figure out the cause. Many theories were explored: allergies, vitamin deficiency, stress, lack of hormones, etc. I was even taken to Children's Hospital for a battery of tests, where they put me in front of 200 medical students to discuss my case. Along with the many theories explored, we also attempted numerous remedies: cortisone injections into the scalp, daily scalp massages, mega-dose vitamins and oils and creams, but I just kept losing more and more hair. By age 13, I was completely bald and finally resorted to wearing wigs. As a young teenage girl, this was an extremely dev- astating event. Kids wondered if I had some contagious disease or if I were dying. Being called "Kojak's daughter" or being asked "Where's your lollipop, baldy?" was no fun either. I either ignored their teasing or laughed with them until I got home, then I cried my eyes out!

The worst part was that wigs weren't made like they are today, so it was obvious that the wig was not my real hair and people always stared at "it" versus looking me in the eyes when talking to me. Fortunately, my Dad and Mom taught me to hold my head high and realize there were other children who had much worse conditions. But as a typical 13-year-old girl who was very active in sports and wanted to rough-house like everyone else, the situa- tion led to some very embarrassing moments. The most embarrassing event in my life involved David Lane. I was totally in love with the 15-year-old, dark-haired, hand- some older brother of one of my church playmates.

On Sunday evenings, the church-group kids all got together and went roller-skating at the local rink. We looked forward to this weekly event because our parents dropped us off for three hours. On this particular Sunday, the "whoopie" was announced 30 minutes early—a game where three people held hands while skating and when "whoopie" was yelled everyone had to change directions. The moment had come! Kimmie and David Lane and I were going to skate together. This meant holding David's hand! I had heart palpitations just thinking of it. Three "whoopies" into it, an out-of-control skater suddenly came straight for me, collided with my head and my wig went flying 50 feet down the skating rink! I was com- pletely mortified as I stood beside David, and he looked at my bald head! The entire skating rink came to a standstill as one of my friends picked up the wig and plunked it back on my head. In her haste she put it on backwards so the long curls were hanging past my nose and the bangs were at my neck! What a sight! I was immediately surrounded by all my friends as they shuffled me off to the ladies' room to fix myself up.

Once I was in that restroom there was no getting me out! I didn't want to feel the stares and hear the questions or, even worse, see David Lane's expression of revulsion! I immediately used the restroom phone, and through passionate sobs, asked my dad to come get me. To this day, Dad says one of the hardest things he has ever done was answering, "No, you wash your face of tears, straighten up your hair, and go skate the rest of the night away." I was completely devastated! My dad had always been my hero. Why wouldn't he come rescue me? Thirty minutes and three pleading phone calls later, the reply was the same, "No, you get back out there and skate."

It was then, as I sat in tears on the bathroom floor, that David Lane appeared. He just skated right into the ladies' room, grabbed my hand and asked me to come back out to skate. I wiped my face, held my head high and skated the rest of the night away with the boy I loved.

A few months later, a young doctor said I had "alopecia" (baldness caused by an allergy to the chemicals released by my own hair follicles). As an allergic reaction, my hair fell out. The doctor said that when I started menstruating, my chemical makeup would change and I would most likely get my hair back! Finally, a name to what was happening and a logical cause! Sure enough, at age 16, I started menstruating and my hair started growing! Within six months, I no longer had to wear a wig.

Today I keep my dark hair very long down to my waist, making up for all those lost years. In fact, when I asked my husband what was the first thing he noticed about me, he sincerely said, "Your long, beautiful, dark hair!"

I have not had contact with David Lane for over 15 years, but if he reads this, I want to tell him and my dad, "Thank you. Your rescue of a 13-year-old bald girl transformed a memory of a most embarrassing moment into a memory of kindness and love."

Debbie Ross-Preston

Money of My Own

"May I help you?" I asked.

It was one of the two jobs I held. But staying in college was worth it. The first job was cold calling, making calls to people's homes, asking them if they wanted a subscription to one magazine or the other. Since the calls were placed between five and 10 at night, most people considered the call an intrusion either on their dinner plans, their family time, or both. But my job at Wolfe's Department Store was a different matter. More like fun than work, here my task was to straighten the rows of beautiful garments made from the most refined fabrics of intricately woven threads and sell them to lovely women with manicured nails and salon-kept hairstyles—women who could afford such things—or who wanted to.

"Oh, I hope so," she said wistfully. She was a pretty woman of about 35. Wearing a yellow sundress and sandals, her long auburn hair hung in soft curls around her shoulders.

"It's my husband's class reunion in six weeks and I want to look absolutely wonderful for him," she said. "Six weeks ago I was here and saw a gorgeous peach-colored silk dress. Only after I tried it on, did I realize how much it cost so I was almost relieved when the style revealed the extra pounds I was still carrying from my pregnancy. But the dress was so pretty, it motivated me to get back in shape, and now that I am, and with the reunion in just a couple of weeks, I told myself I better start shopping for a dress to wear. I was hoping that I'd find that dress, though I can't imagine that such an exquisite dress would still be here, but maybe, I thought, just maybe. Or, you might have something like it."

I said, "Let's look around to see if the dress is still here." We walked through the four rows of racks of perfectly hung clothes, but the dress she was looking for was nowhere in sight. I could tell by her body language that she was really disappointed.

Her heavy exhale was as lengthy as her deeply drawn inhale. "Oh gosh," she said, obviously let down.

"Last week we received a new shipment of silk dresses," I said encouragingly, trying as much to please and appease her as to be helpful. "They're over here, if you'd like to look at them. Maybe we can find something similar, or maybe one you'll like even better." I led her to the rack of new dresses that had just come in. She looked through them slowly, carefully touching the delicate fabrics with her long graceful fingers.

"Oh," she lamented, as she looked over the elegant apparel, "you should have seen *that* dress." Her eyes widened with her smile. She began to look around at other things, but still enchanted by the special dress she had seen some weeks back, continued to describe it in great detail. Suddenly, it occurred to me that we just might have a couple of these dresses still in the store. Several items had been moved to another department to make room for the new shipment of things in ours.

"What size do you wear?" I asked.

"Size 6," she answered.

"If you don't mind waiting," I said, "I'll have a look in another department. I'll be right back."

When I returned, I found her sitting in a chair, patiently waiting for me. It was clear that the peach-colored silk dress with the cloth-covered buttons was the dress of her choice, and she would wait. When she saw me coming with the very dress she had described, she stood up, and with a look of amazement on her face, covered her mouth with both hands.

"Oh," she said excitedly. "That's it! That's the dress!"

"Size 6!" I said, gleefully holding it out to her. "And, it's on sale, 40 percent off!"

The woman could hardly believe her good fortune. She took the dress and quickly disappeared into the dressing room. Moments later, she emerged to observe herself in the full-length mirror. Slowly she turned to observe herself from every angle, carefully scrutinizing the image in the mirror before her. She was right, the dress was absolutely beautiful, and she looked resplendent in it. But it was more than the transformation of the dress from the frame of the hanger to the frame of her body. She felt lovely and elegant in the dress, and her face radiated her joy. She looked at me, and smiled. No words needed to be exchanged. It was obvious the designer had a woman such as she in mind when it was fashioned.

"Thank you, thank you so much . . . ," she squinted to read the print on my gold name tag—"Bettie, and, oh, by the way, my name is Molly."

Molly paid for the dress in cash; carefully unwrapping a bundle mostly of small bills, counting out the exact amount needed for the dress, then, laying it on the counter. I wrapped up her beautiful new dress and put it in an elegant shopping bag. As I handed it to her, Molly reached out her hand to touch mine, and in a soft, sincere voice said,

"Thank you so much again for all of your help, Bettie. I'm so happy you found this dress for me. I can't wait to wear it."

I was even more sure that when I was married I would take delight in doing things to be special for my husband as she had for hers. It also dawned on me that helping others feel so happy was a better way to earn a living than interrupting someone's dinner plans and family time with magazine sales.

The idea was short-lived.

One evening a few days later, a very handsome man came up to my counter. He tossed a Wolfe's shopping bag on the desk and barked, "This is a return." Through pursed lips, he added, "For cash."

I opened the bag and there lay a beautiful silk size 6 peach-colored dress. I flipped the tag over, and in my handwriting were the store code numbers, the date of the sale, and my register code.

"All the tags are still on it," a woman's voice said softly. I looked up, and there, standing several feet behind him, stood Molly, looking meek and embarrassed. I didn't understand.

"Oh," I said, surprised that the dress was being returned. "Is there something wrong with this dress? If so, we have an alteration department that can fix it for you."

"No, there's nothing wrong with the dress," the man shot back. "No one in her right mind would pay this much for a dress." He went on to say other things, too, all designed for intimidation.

I made the exchange—her dress for her carefully saved money. The man took "his" money, shoved it into his pocket and ordered, "C'mon, let's get out of here." He led the way as they left.

The incident seemed like a scene in a movie that's out of sequence and doesn't quite belong. Incomplete, like a puzzle that's missing just one last piece; like falling hail in a rainstorm on a hot sunny summer's day, like a Christmas tree with a star but no lights or ornaments, or someone showing up at a formal banquet in a bathing suit. It just didn't fit. In the short time I'd helped Molly, I'd seen only her beauty, her gentle nature and genuine desire to please her husband. Knowing little else, I assumed the recipient of such love would behave in a way that merited such treatment—would even treat the giver in a like manner.

Thoughts of that incident haunted me for several days. It seemed so abrupt, so unjust. My first thoughts centered around how I would feel if this had happened to me. I concluded that not only would I earn my own money in life, but make my own decisions, as well.

Still unable to put the incident out of my mind, I wondered if he knew how much thought had gone into her purchase. If only he knew the loving actions that went with the purchase, perhaps then he might have let her keep the dress, or handled the situation differently—or at least treated his wife differently. Then again, perhaps he wouldn't.

The following weeks, I saw that the dress was marked down even further. Each time my eyes caught sight of it, I felt a sense of disquiet.

While alphabetizing the returned merchandise slips from our department for the store's accounting office several days later, I came upon the couple's return receipt. As though it were an omen of some kind, the man's telephone number stood out. Deciding it was a small risk, I called the man at his work.

"Sir," I said, "I hope I'm not disturbing you. I'm the salesclerk who waited on you and your wife when you came in to return a dress she had purchased."

"Yes, I remember you," came the disgruntled reply. "What do you need?"

"I may be out of line here," I began, "but, well, your wife made such an impression on me, and I thought you ought to know . . ." the line remained silent so I continued, "what a truly beautiful woman she is and not only in her outward appearance, but in the love and devotion she portrays to you and your new son. I could tell you weren't happy about the money she had spent on that dress, but it seemed so important to your wife to look beautiful for you and make you proud of her at your reunion, and she was so pleased to find the price had been substantially discounted." Drawing a deep breath, I continued, "She honestly bought it with you in mind, and now the dress has just been marked down even further. Can't you let her have it?" I pleaded.

It seemed so logical and simple to me. In a last effort to convey my message, I added, "I guess what I'm trying to say is something my father taught me when he said, 'It's good to value the things money can buy, but it's good, too, to check up once in a while and make sure you haven't lost the precious things in life that money can't buy.'"

My hopes rose at what I saw as a thoughtful silence, before being crushed when he answered, "You're right, you're out of line. And I think I made my intentions clear when I was in the store. But thanks for thinking of us." With that, he hung up. No "good-bye," just the harsh click of the phone—our communication severed.

Having been so thoroughly dismissed, I felt discounted, like an uneducated schoolgirl working in a clothing store. These feelings didn't find a home for long; I'd known the risk before calling; I expressed my feelings. I wanted him to know what I thought. He was the one who was emotionally illiterate here, not me. It was worth the call—even though I wished things could have turned out differently.

When I came to work a couple of days later, I was greeted by a bouquet of white daisies with a note that read, "Thank you for your thoughtfulness." The card held no signature.

"When did this arrive?" I asked Helen, my coworker.

"Yesterday," she responded.

"Do you have any idea who they're from?"

"We assumed you had a secret admirer!"

Puzzled, I went about my work as usual.

I was rehanging some apparel when an excited, vaguely familiar voice said, "I was hoping I'd find you here!"

"Oh, it's good to see you again Molly," I said, surprised. Why hadn't I put it together? Of course the daisies had been from her, a peace offering for her husband's rudeness.

"He bought it for me!" she said gleefully. She didn't have any doubts that I'd remember what "it" was, as her words seem to burst forth in her obvious delight.

Pleasantly stunned by her words, I found myself grinning as widely as she was. "Oh, I'm so happy for you—the dress was made for you!"

"But that's not all," she went on, unfastening her purse to retrieve something even as she spoke. "In fact, it's not even the best part. I just had to show you—look at the note he put in with it when he gave it to me." Unconsciously touching it to her heart, as if it were infinitely precious to her, she then thrust the note toward me, obviously eager to share her joy.

Unfolding it carefully, my smile at her happiness still in place, I read the note's bold handwriting.

> *Darling,*
>
> *I'm sorry that I've let the pressure of my work and being a good provider cause me to lose sight of just what it is I'm working for. I'm also sorry it took me this long to realize how much you deserve this dress. It's taken me too long to realize a lot of things—including how*

beautiful you'll look wearing it. And most importantly,
I've realized just how lucky I am to have you, and your
love. Thank you for loving me as you do.

Yours Forever,
XOXOXO

I felt her watch me as I read it silently, and yet, it was
her eyes that were moist with tears. She was no doubt,
rereading it with her heart, each word memorized, forever
etched in her heart. The fullness of her heart touched me
as much as the humility and love in the words of his note.

"That's wonderful, Molly," I said, really meaning it.

"I thought so too," she replied. "I just had to let you
know. Hey, lovely flowers," she said gazing at the daisies
sitting next to the cash register. "Are they from your
boyfriend?" Not waiting for a reply, she continued, "You
know, my husband sent me a bouquet of roses yesterday.
Oh, I just love that man."

I said nothing. There seemed something wise in my
decision not to tell her about the call I made to her husband—or the white daisies he had sent me for the wake-
up call—thanking me for reminding him how special he
was to her.

Hearts at work. Amazing aren't they?

Bettie B. Youngs
Excerpted from **Gifts of the Heart**

2

ON
KINDNESS

*Spread love everywhere you go: First of all in
your own house . . . let no one ever come to
you without leaving better and happier.
Be the living expression of God's kindness;
kindness in your face, kindness in your eyes,
kindness in your smile, kindness in your
warm greeting.*

Mother Teresa

Hi, Cornelius

To cultivate kindness is a valuable part of the business of life.

Samuel Johnson

I had been writing a newspaper column for almost 20 years. As part of my work I had seen some of the darkest and unhappiest aspects of human nature, and I had written about them. It was beginning to get to me.

There were nights when I would go home from work and question the very nature of humanity, and wonder if there was any answer to the unremitting cruelty I was observing and writing about so often. Part of this had to do with a particular case I had been covering. The case involved one of the worst crimes I had ever encountered.

A beautiful, bright-eyed, four-year-old boy named Lattie McGee had been systematically tortured over the course of a long Chicago summer. He had been beaten, he had been starved, he had been hanged upside down in a locked and darkened closet for nights on end.

All that summer his life dwindled agonizingly away in that closet, and no one knew he was there; no one heard his muffled cries. After his death, when the police discovered what had been done to him, I wrote column after column about the people who had murdered him. So many cases of impoverished children from forgotten neighborhoods get lost in the court system. I wanted to make sure that Lattie McGee received justice, or something close to it.

With all the public interest in Lattie because of the columns, the story of his brother, whose name was Cornelius Abraham, did not receive as much attention. The same things that were done to Lattie were done to Cornelius, too. Somehow he survived. He watched his brother slowly being killed and was unable to stop the killers. Cornelius' brave testimony in court is what helped to convict them.

By the end of the trial Cornelius had just turned nine. He was a thin, extremely quiet boy; with his little brother dead and his mother and her boyfriend in prison, he was living with other relatives. The two great loves of his life were reading and basketball.

In one of the columns I had written about Lattie, I had mentioned Cornelius' passion for basketball. Steve Schanwald, a vice president of the Chicago Bulls, had read the column and left a message at my office. Though tickets to Bulls' games were without exception sold out, Schanwald said that if Cornelius would like to come to a game he would be sure there were tickets available. Jim Bigoness, the Cook County assistant state's attorney who had delicately prepared Cornelius' testimony for the trial, and I took him to the game.

To every Chicago youngster who follows basketball, the stadium was a shrine. Think of where Cornelius once was, locked up and tormented and hurt. And now he was in the stadium, about to see his first Bulls game.

We walked down a stairway, until we were in a lower-level hallway. Cornelius stood between us. Then a door opened and a man came out. Cornelius looked up, and his eyes filled with a combination of wonder and awe and total disbelief.

Cornelius tried to say something; his mouth was moving but no words would come out. He tried to speak and then the man helped him out by speaking first.

"Hi, Cornelius," the man said. "I'm Michael Jordan."

Jordan knelt down and spoke quietly with Cornelius. He made some jokes and told some stories about basketball and he didn't rush. You have to understand—for a long time the only adults Cornelius had any contact with were adults who wanted to hurt and humiliate him. And now Michael Jordan was saying, "Are you going to cheer for us today? We're going to need it."

Jordan went back into the locker room to finish dressing for the game. Bigoness and I walked Cornelius back upstairs to the court. There was one more surprise waiting.

Cornelius was given a red shirt of the kind worn by the Bulls' ball boys. He retrieved balls for the players from both teams as they warmed up.

Then, as the game was about to begin, he was led to Jordan's seat on the Bulls' bench. That's where he was going to sit—right next to Jordan's seat. During the minutes of the game when Jordan was out and resting, Cornelius would be sitting with him; when Jordan was on the court, Cornelius would be saving his seat for him. At one point late in the game Jordan took a pass and sailed into the air and slammed home a basket. And there, just a few feet away, was Cornelius Abraham, laughing out loud with joy.

I wanted to thank Jordan for taking the time to be so nice to Cornelius. The meeting between them, I had learned, had been something that Jordan had volunteered for; he had been aware of the Lattie McGee case, and when he had heard that the Bulls were giving Cornelius tickets to the game, he had let it be known that he was available.

After the game, in the locker room after the last sports-writer left, Jordan got up to retrieve his gym bag and head for home. As he walked toward the door of the locker room he saw me and stopped, and I said, "I just wanted to tell you how much Cornelius appreciated what you did for him."

For a second I had the strange but undeniable impression that perhaps this was a man who didn't get thanked all that often—or at least that there were so many people endlessly lining up to beseech him for one thing or another that all he was accustomed to was the long file of faces in front of him wanting an autograph, a favor, a moment of his time, faces that would immediately be replaced by more faces with more entreaties. He stood there waiting, as if he was so used to ceaselessly being asked for things that he thought my thanks on Cornelius' behalf might be the inevitable preface to petitioning him for something else.

When I didn't say anything, he said, "That's why you came back down here?"

"Well, I don't think you know how much today meant to Cornelius," I said.

"No, I'm just surprised that you came back down to tell me," he said.

"My mom would kill me if I didn't," I said, smiling. "She tried to raise me right."

He smiled back, "Mine, too," he said.

We shook hands and I turned to leave and I heard him say, "Do you come out to a lot of games?"

"First one," I said.

"Well, you ought to come back," he said.

Bob Greene

Changed Lives

In 1921, Lewis Lawes became the warden at Sing Sing Prison. No prison was tougher than Sing Sing during that time. But when Warden Lawes retired some 20 years later, that prison had become a humanitarian institution. Those who studied the system said credit for the change belonged to Lawes. But when he was asked about the transformation, here's what he said: "I owe it all to my wonderful wife, Catherine, who is buried outside the prison walls."

Catherine Lawes was a young mother with three small children when her husband became the warden. Every - body warned her from the beginning that she should never set foot inside the prison walls, but that didn't stop Catherine! When the first prison basketball game was held, she went . . . walking into the gym with her three beautiful kids and she sat in the stands with the inmates.

Her attitude was: "My husband and I are going to take care of these men and I believe they will take care of me! I don't have to worry!"

She insisted on getting acquainted with them and their records. She discovered one convicted murderer was blind so she paid him a visit. Holding his hand in hers she said, "Do you read Braille?"

"What's Braille?" he asked. Then she taught him how to read. Years later he would weep in love for her.

Later, Catherine found a deaf-mute in prison. She went to school to learn how to use sign language. Many said that Catherine Lawes was the body of Jesus that came alive again in Sing Sing from 1921 to 1937.

Then, she was killed in a car accident. The next morning Lewis Lawes didn't come to work, so the acting warden took his place. It seemed almost instantly that the prison knew something was wrong.

The following day, her body was resting in a casket in her home, three-quarters of a mile from the prison. As the acting warden took his early morning walk, he was shocked to see a large crowd of the toughest, hardest-looking criminals gathered like a herd of animals at the main gate. He came closer and noted tears of grief and sadness. He knew how much they loved Catherine. He turned and faced the men, "All right, men, you can go. Just be sure and check in tonight!" Then he opened the gate and a parade of criminals walked, without a guard, the three-quarters of a mile to stand in line to pay their final respects to Catherine Lawes. And every one of them checked back in. Every one!

Tim Kimmel

Directory Assistance

You have not lived a perfect day, even though you have earned your money, unless you have done something for someone who will never be able to repay you.

Ruth Smeltzer

Although my sister was sure Daddy would be okay, I worried as I called the hospital. My husband at the time was out of town at a radio advertising convention. "If you need me, call the radio station. The secretary has the name of the hotel and the number," he said before he left.

I waited until mid-morning to call Memorial Hospital in northern Indiana. The moment I heard Jane's voice, I knew Daddy was in trouble. "He's filling up with fluid. The doctor here can't do any more for him. An ambulance has been ordered, and then he'll be transported to St. John's. They have more cardio equipment there." Jane continued, "Mom and I are going to grab lunch and then drive from Memorial to St. John's. There's nothing more we can do here."

"Should I come?"

"Not yet. He's stable. Why don't you wait."

The rest of the morning inched by. I tried to work. I collected ads, wrote them up and turned them in. Close to noon, I called St. John's. The nurse in cardio checked her records. The transport had left but returned to Memorial and never reached St. John's. That was all she could tell me.

There was only one reason the transport would have turned back. Daddy must have died en route. I dialed Memorial, my mind racing. Should I drive immediately to Indiana? My family was five hours away. Should I call for my husband and wait for him? If Daddy was dead, did it matter?

The nurse who answered was a friend of my sister. Because Jane worked at Memorial as a respiratory therapist, many of the nursing staff knew her and, therefore, knew about Daddy.

"What happened?" I asked.

She stuttered around. Hospital regulations forbid her from saying, but she recommended I get in touch with my sister as soon as possible.

"I can't!" I wailed. "I'm in Illinois. You have to tell me. It's cruel not to be honest. All I'm asking is . . . is . . . is he dead?"

Yes, of course, he was. He had died two blocks from Memorial en route to St. John's Hospital. Now, in my grief, I had to decide what to do about traveling.

I called the radio station. "Do you have the number of Jim's hotel?" They put me on hold. They couldn't find it. They were sorry.

With shaking hands, I opened the phone book. The area code for Kansas City was 913. I dialed information. Bell Telephone policy allowed operators to give out three phone numbers for each directory assistance inquiry. I jotted down the three numbers of the first hotel chains I could think of.

I called one. Neither the radio convention nor my husband was there. I called the second—same situation. I called the third. Again, I struck out. I redialed directory assistance. This time I could only think of the name of one more hotel chain, the Hyatt. I wrote down the number, and then I dialed. The numbness had started wearing off, and I sniffled a little into the receiver.

"No, we don't have a convention for radio ad managers here, and your husband's name doesn't show on our list of registered guests," said the switchboard operator. "Sorry, I'm just the operator . . ."

But before she could hang up, a sob escaped my lips. After a long silence, I clutched the receiver in my hand and wiped my nose on the back of my sleeve.

"What's wrong?" she asked quietly.

"My dad died a few minutes ago. He—his body—is in Indiana. It's a five-hour trip, and I can't find my husband. I don't know whether to jump in the car and go or to wait," I blurted. "I want to be with my sisters and my mom, but I don't know what to do!"

Another long silence. Then she spoke slowly and quietly, "Give me your name and your number and sit tight until I call back." Gratefully, I did. She called me back in less than five minutes.

"Joanna, I found him. He's at the Adam's Mark Hotel. I've notified the manager, and they have people posted to grab him as soon as the general session breaks. That should be within 20 minutes. It's impossible for him to get past them."

I sobbed into the phone. "Thank you, thank you so much."

"One more thing," she continued, "if you do decide to drive, please take a friend. Be careful. You've had a dreadful shock and . . . and . . . be careful, okay? I'm sorry about your dad."

From another state, the voice of a friend soothed me. Whoever this woman was, she was more than just a switchboard operator. She was a wonderful, kind person who was more than her job.

Joanna Slan

A Christmas Story

After the verb "To Love" . . . "To Help" is the most beautiful verb in the world.

Bertha von Suttner

During the Roosevelt era, times were tough. The president was promising a brighter moon, but the Beasleys hadn't seen it rise over their small town in the Texas panhandle.

So when he got the call that his son was ill in California and not expected to live, Bill Beasley didn't know how he was going to scrape together the money for his wife and himself to make the trip. Bill had worked as a trucker his entire life, but he never managed to accumulate any savings. Swallowing his pride, he phoned a few close relatives for help, but they were no better off.

So it was with embarrassment and dejection that Bill Beasley walked the mile from his house to the filling station and told the owner, "The son is really sick," he said, "and I've got no cash. Can you trust me for the phone call to California?"

"Pick up the phone and talk as long as you need to," was the reply. As he started to dial, he was interrupted by a voice asking, "Aren't you Bill Beasley?"

It was a stranger, jumping down from the cab of a truck with out-of-state plates. The young man didn't look familiar, and Bill could only stare at him with a puzzled look and say, "That's right, I am."

"Your son was one of my best pals when we were growing up together. When I went off to college, I lost all track of him." He paused for a moment and then continued. "Heard you say he's sick?"

"Real bad, from what we hear. I'm gonna call and try to make some arrangements for the wife to get out there with him." Then, as a matter of courtesy, he added, "Have yourself a Merry Christmas. Wish your daddy was still with us."

Old man Beasley walked into the office of the station and placed his call to the cousin on the West coast, informing him that he or his wife hoped to be out as soon as possible.

There was an obvious look of sorrow on the elder citizen's face as he assured the owner that he would pay for the call as soon as he could.

"The call has been paid for. That trucker—the one your son used to pal around with—left me a 20 and said to give you the change when the phone bill comes in. He also left you this envelope."

The old man fumbled open the envelope and pulled out two sheets of paper. One read, "You were the first trucker I ever traveled with, the first my dad trusted enough to let me go along with when I was barely five years old. I remember you bought me a Snickers bar." The second sheet, much smaller in size, was a signed check with an attached message: "Fill out the amount needed for you and your wife to make the trip . . . and give your son, my pal, a Snickers bar. Merry Christmas!"

Author Unknown

Cold Hands

We cannot live only for ourselves. A thousand fibers connect us with our fellow men!

Herman Melville

I was cleaning out the pockets of my six-year-old's winter coat, when I found a pair of mittens in each pocket. Thinking that one pair must not be enough to keep her hands warm, I asked her why she was carrying two pairs of mittens in her coat. She replied, "I've been doing that for a long time, Mom. You see, some kids come to school without mittens and if I carry another pair, I can share with them and then their hands won't get cold."

Joyce Andresen

The Woodwork Angel

Men are rich only as they give. He who gives great service gets great returns.

Elbert Hubbard

My teeth screamed. I couldn't neglect them any longer. I finally ignored my fear of dentists and decided to get them fixed. But how? I was a college sophomore and barely supported myself with part-time jobs.

Maybe I could fix the worst one. I flipped open the Yellow Pages and called the first dentist within walking distance. The receptionist told me to come right over. As I hurried across the campus, I forgot the pain in worrying about how I would pay the bill.

In a few minutes I was in a chair being examined by a dentist who said, "Hmm!" as he surveyed the wreckage of my mouth. "Your teeth are in bad shape."

"I already know that," I snapped, in a smart-aleck way to hide my fear.

"But don't worry, I'm going to fix them."

"No, you're not. I can't afford to pay you." I started climbing out of the chair.

"What are you doing?"

"I told you, I have no money."

"You're a student at the university, aren't you?"

What difference did that make? "Yes . . ."

"You're going to graduate in a few years, aren't you?"

"I hope so."

"And then you expect to get a job, don't you?"

"That's my plan."

"Well, then you'll pay me. Meantime, you concentrate on your classes and leave the dentistry to me."

I stared at him. He really meant it. He calmly picked up his tools and fixed the aching cavity.

From that day on, I saw him every week until my teeth were in good shape. And he kept them that way with regular checkups. After graduation, I got a job and settled his bill in a few months.

In the 40 years following, I've learned to call this man a "woodwork angel." These are strangers who appear out of nowhere—out of the woodwork—when I need help. They've lent and given me money, materials or equipment; they've taught me skills and helped me organize groups; sometimes they've rescued me from danger or making a big mistake. So, dentist dear, wherever you are, bless you and thank you again!

Varda One

The 11th Box

It is more blessed to give than to receive.

Acts 20:35

What is your most memorable Thanksgiving? For me, it was on the eve of the day. The church had the names of 10 families scheduled to receive food baskets. A local merchant donated hams, and groceries were purchased from the food bank. As we packed the boxes in the fellowship hall, these families were excited over the food they were taking home. It would be the best meal many had enjoyed in months. As they were picking up their boxes, another family arrived. Father, mother and three children piled out of an old pickup truck and came inside the hall. This was a new family, not on our list. They had just heard there was food being distributed by a church.

I explained that we did not have enough for an extra family. And as I tried to assure them that I would do what I could, an amazing thing happened. With no prompting, a woman put down the box she was carrying and quickly found an empty box to place beside it. She began removing items from her box to share. Soon others followed her lead, and these poor people created an 11th box for the new family.

Pastor Bill Simpson
Submitted by M'Shel Bowen

The Sandwich Man

The capacity to care is the thing that gives life its deepest meaning and significance.

Pablo Casals

What would you do if you wanted to make a difference in the world, leave a mark or put a deposit on a ticket into heaven? Would you think big and pick the flashiest or most grandiose of acts? Or would you quietly persevere every day, doing one personal deed at a time?

Michael Christiano, a New York City court officer, rises every morning at 4 A.M., in good and bad weather, workday or holiday, and walks into his sandwich shop. No, he doesn't own a deli, it's really his personal kitchen. In it are the fixings of his famous sandwiches, famous only to those who desperately need them to stave off hunger for the day. By 5:50 A.M., he's making the rounds of the makeshift homeless shelters on Centre and Lafayette Streets, near New York's City Hall. In a short time, he gives out 200 sandwiches to as many homeless people as he can, before beginning his work day in the courthouse.

It started 20 years ago with a cup of coffee and a roll for a homeless man named John. Day after day, Michael brought John sandwiches, tea, clothes, and when it was really cold, a resting place in his car while he worked. In the beginning, Michael just wanted to do a good deed.

But one day a voice in his head compelled him to do more. On this cold, winter morning, he asked John if he would like to get cleaned up. It was an empty offer, because Michael was sure John would refuse. Unexpectedly, John said, "Are you gonna wash me?"

Michael heard an inner voice say, *Put your money where your mouth is.* Looking at this poor man, covered in ragged and smelly clothes, unkempt, hairy and wild-looking, Michael was afraid. But he also knew that he was looking at a big test of his commitment. So he helped John upstairs to the locker room of the courthouse to begin the work.

John's body was a mass of cuts and sores, the result of years of pain and neglect. His right hand had been amputated, and Michael pushed through his own fears and revulsion. He helped John wash, cut his hair, shaved him and shared breakfast with him. "It was at that moment," Michael remembers, "that I *knew* I had a calling, and I believed that I had it within me to do anything."

With the idea for his sandwiches born, Michael began his calling. He receives no corporate sponsorship, saying, "I'm not looking for an act of charity that goes in the record books or gets media attention. I just want to do good, day by day, in my small way. Sometimes it comes out of my pocket, sometimes I get help. But this is really something that *I* can do, one day and one person at a time.

"There are days when it's snowing," he says, "and I have a hard time leaving my warm bed and the comfort of my family to go downtown with sandwiches. But then that voice in me starts chattering, and I get to it."

And get to it he does. Michael has made 200 sand-wiches every day for the past 20 years. "When I give out sandwiches," Michael explains, "I don't simply lay them on a table for folks to pick up. I look everyone in the eye, shake their hands, and I offer them my wishes for a good and hopeful day. Each person is important to me. I don't see them as 'the homeless,' but as people who need food, an encouraging smile and some positive human contact.

"Once Mayor Koch turned up to make the rounds with me. He didn't invite the media, it was just us," says Michael. But of all Michael's memories, working side by side with the Mayor was not as important as working next to someone else . . .

A man had disappeared from the ranks of the sandwich takers, and Michael thought about him from time to time. He hoped the man had moved on to more comfortable conditions. One day, the man showed up, transformed, greeting Michael clean, warmly clothed, shaven and carry-ing sandwiches of his own to hand out. Michael's daily dose of fresh food, warm handshakes, eye contact and well wishes had given this man the hope and encouragement he so desperately needed. Being seen every day as a per-son, not as a category, had turned this man's life around.

The moment needed no dialogue. The two men worked silently, side by side, handing out their sandwiches. It was another day on the streets of New York, but a day with just a little more hope.

Meladee McCarty

Don't Pass Me By

At different stages in our lives, the signs of love may vary: dependence, attraction, contentment, worry, loyalty, grief, but at heart, the source is always the same. Human beings have the rare capacity to connect with each other, against all odds.

Michael Dorris

He walked with eyes lowered, head to the ground.
When he saw me, he spoke, and I took in his sight.
He was scruffy and raggedy
in his eyes was no light.
He said, "Ma'am, I'm hungry."
He was very polite.

I said to him softly, "No money have I,
but I'll buy you some food with these food stamps of
    mine."
We walked on in silence, this homeless old man,
and he said, "Give me your number—
I'll pay you back when I can."

I looked in his eyes, where hopelessness lay,
and I said, "Never mind. I don't want you to pay."
As we walked down the aisles of the grocery store,
like a child he picked something, then asked for some
      more.
I gladly told him to fill all his needs,
because in my lifetime, I've done some bad deeds.

I'll never forget him, as he went on his way,
because he gave me something I can never repay.
He gave me a chance to give what I could,
a chance to show love to the misunderstood—
a chance to feed someone when no one else would—
a chance to be special, a chance to be good.

I'll ever be grateful to the stranger in rags,
for showing me Love in a few grocery bags,
for letting me be the one who had more,
for letting me answer his knock at my door.

You see, I'm no angel, though I've wanted to be.
I've hurt many people by just being me,
and this man, this stranger, who did not pass me by,
set free for an instant an angel to fly.

Jude Revoli

Bidding from the Heart

*It is one of the beautiful compensations of this
life that no one can sincerely try to help another
without helping himself.*

Ralph Waldo Emerson

Jayne Fisher watched anxiously as her 17-year-old
daughter Katie pulled her unruly lamb into the arena of
the Madison County Junior Livestock sale. With luck,
Katie wouldn't collapse, as she had during a livestock
show the day before.

Katie was battling cancer. This was her first chance in
months to be outdoors having fun, away from hospitals
and chemotherapy treatments, and she had come with
high hopes for earning some sizable spending money. She
had wavered a little on her decision to part with the lamb,
but with lamb averaging two dollars a pound, Katie was
looking forward to a lot more than pin money. So she centered the lamb for viewing, and the bidding began.

That's when Roger Wilson, the auctioneer, had a sudden inspiration that brought some unexpected results.
"We sort of let folks know that Katie had a situation that

wasn't too pleasant," is how he tells it. He hoped that his introduction would push the bidding up, at least a little bit.

Well, the lamb sold for $11.50 a pound, but things didn't stop there. The buyer paid up, then decided to give the lamb back so that it could be sold again.

That started a chain reaction, with families buying the animal and giving it back, over and over again. When local businesses started buying and returning, the earnings really began to pile up. The first sale is the only one Katie's mom remembers. After that, she was crying too hard as the crowd kept shouting, "Resell! Resell!"

Katie's lamb was sold 36 times that day, and the last buyer gave it back for good. Katie ended up with more than $16,000 for a fund to pay her medical expenses—and she still got to keep her famous lamb.

Rita Price

Ask for the Moon and Get It

When you give of yourself, you receive more than you give.

Antoine de Saint-Exupéry

As I grew up and went into business, I always had a soft spot for kids without bikes. When I was in my 20s, I lived next door to a little boy that I liked. And, wouldn't you know, his parents couldn't afford to buy him a bike. So one Saturday, I went to the local hardware store and blew half a paycheck, $25.00 for a surprise. You should have seen that kid jump up and down—he was my friend for life. But this is not the end of the story.

Over the years, as I saved money and became affluent, I gave away bike after bike—about 100 in all, up to the year 1977.

Then in 1977, I was looking for a way to brighten the lives of underprivileged children in Minneapolis. I decided to throw a Christmas party for them—a gala get-together for more than 1,000 impoverished kids of all races who never owned a bike. I would serve them refreshments in a large auditorium, I would tell them they could succeed, as I had. I would give them silver dollars as symbols of a richer future. And I would give them bicycles—a shiny new bike for each and every kid.

My assistants and I hid the bikes behind a gigantic curtain. Then when the celebration reached a climax, the curtain went up. You should have heard the gasps, the shouts, the cheers, the gleeful screaming as those kids gazed upon 1,050 brand-spanking-new two-wheelers neatly parked in rows. Then they scrambled toward the bikes, touching them, sitting on them, riding them around joyfully.

Like Martin Luther King Jr., I, too, have a dream. I'd like to give another bicycle party before I die—this one somewhere in the Middle East. I'd invite children from Israel, Egypt, Iran, Syria, Lebanon and other countries in that eye-for-an-eye region that breeds so much distrust and terrorism. There will be gifts, games and a bicycle for each child; but the biggest gift will be a demonstration of youthful brotherhood. The relationship between young Jews and young Arabs will determine the kind of Middle East that emerges in the next generation.

Such a party would involve sensitive negotiations and would be very difficult to stage without incident. I'll have to do a lot of pushing and a lot of asking to pull it off, but I'm more than willing. In fact, I'm determined.

Why? Because I know what it's like to grow up in a world of poverty, distrust, prejudice and pain.

One time I asked for a job shining shoes and was turned away. I was nine when the exclusive Miscowaubik Club was looking for a boy to shine shoes at a nickel a pair. My mother dressed me in my best clothes. I remember my dad even dressed up before taking me there. My father drove me in his horse-drawn junk wagon. I remember even now how nervous I was sitting beside him on the high, wooden seat. We didn't talk much and I've often wondered if he was quiet that day because he suspected what might happen when I knocked on the door of the club. Its members were the wealthiest families in town, the captains and lieutenants of the Calumet and Hecia Consolidated Copper Mining Company. Even the name of the company awed and intimidated me.

As I sat on the wooden seat beside my father, jostling up and down, I saw the Miscowaubik Club come into view. It was imposing and yet elegant. My father waited while I walked to the big front door; I remember the brass handle on it. With beating heart and high hopes, I knocked. The door opened, and a well-dressed man, probably the manager, peered down at me. He didn't invite me in. He just asked what I wanted. I said, "My name is Percy Ross, and I've heard you need someone to shine shoes." He replied coolly, "We don't need boys like you."

The words hit me like a ton of bricks. Dazed, I walked back to the horse and wagon. My father was so quiet, so very quiet. I didn't know what to think at the time. Why was I turned away? Maybe it was because I was Jewish. Maybe it was because I was from the other side of the tracks: painted in large letters on the side of my father's wagon were the words WM. ROSS—JUNK DEALER.

On the ride home, the horse's hooves hit the street like hammers on my soul. I asked my father, "Why didn't he let me in the door? What kind of boy am I?" My father didn't have any answers. I remember I cried all the way home.

I have gotten over many disappointments, rebuffs and injuries in my life, but the wound I received that day still hurts. It is this wound that sparked the dream of having a bicycle party in the Middle East.

I'm going to give that party for the hope, however faint, of a world without hate, fear, oppression or resignation. I think it can make a difference.

Percy Ross

Passing on Small Change

I believe it is the nature of people to be heroes, given a chance.

James A. Autry

The pharmacist handed me my prescription, apologized for the wait, and explained that his register had already closed. He asked if I would mind using the register at the front of the store.

I told him not to worry and walked up front, where one person was in line ahead of me, a little girl no more than seven, with a bottle of Children's Motrin on the counter. She clenched a little green and white striped coin purse closely to her chest.

The purse reminded me of the days when, as a child, I played dress-up in my grandma's closet. I'd march around the house in oversized clothes, drenched in costume jewelry and hats and scarves, talking "grownup talk" to anyone who would listen. I remembered the thrill one day when I gave a pretend dollar to someone, and he handed back some real coins for me to put into my special purse. "Keep the change!" he told me with a wink.

Now the clerk rang up the little girl's medicine, while she shakily pulled out a coupon, a dollar bill and some coins. I watched her blush as she tried to count her money, and I could see right away that she was about a dollar short. With a quick wink to the checker, I slipped a dollar bill onto the counter and signaled the clerk to ring up the sale. The child scooped her uncounted change into her coin purse, grabbed her package and scurried out the door.

As I headed to my car, I felt a tug on my shirt. There was the girl, looking up at me with her big brown eyes. She gave me a grin, wrapped her arms around my legs for a long moment then stretched out her little hand. It was full of coins. "Thank you," she whispered.

"That's okay," I answered. I flashed her a smile and winked, "Keep the change!"

Nancy Mitchell

Big Feet—Bigger Heart

When deeds speak, words are nothing.

African Proverb

It was an unseasonably hot day. Everybody it seemed, was looking for some kind of relief, so an ice cream store was a natural place to stop.

A little girl, clutching her money tightly, entered the store. Before she could say a word, the store clerk sharply told her to get outside and read the sign on the door, and stay out until she put on some shoes. She left slowly, and a big man followed her out of the store.

He watched as she stood in front of the store and read the sign: No Bare Feet. Tears started rolling down her cheeks as she turned and walked away. Just then the big man called to her. Sitting down on the curb, he took off his size-12 shoes, and set them in front of the girl saying, "Here, you won't be able to walk in these, but if you sort of slide along, you can get your ice cream cone."

Then he lifted the little girl up and set her feet into the shoes. "Take your time," he said, "I get tired of moving them around, and it'll feel good to just sit here and eat my ice cream." The shining eyes of the little girl could not be missed as she shuffled up to the counter and ordered her ice cream cone.

He was a big man, all right. Big belly, big shoes, but most of all, he had a big heart.

Anonymous
From Brian Cavanaugh's The Sower's Seeds

Winning

I believe every person has a heart and if you can reach it, you can make a difference.

Uli Derickson

His mother told us the story the day after.

Kenneth was in junior high school and was excited and eager about participating in a day of Special Olympics events. While his parents watched expectantly from the stands, he ran, and won, the first race. He was proud of his ribbon and the cheers from the crowd.

He ran in the second race. Just at the finish line, when he again would have won, he stopped, then stepped off the track. His parents gently questioned him. "Why did you do that, Kenneth? If you had continued running, you would have won another race."

Kenneth innocently replied, "But, Mom, I already have a ribbon. Billy didn't have a ribbon yet."

Clifford and Jerie Furness

Goodness Defies the Odds

It is raining still. . . . Maybe it is not one of those showers that is here one minute and gone the next, as I had so boldly assumed. Maybe none of them are. After all, life in itself is a chain of rainy days. But there are times when not all of us have umbrellas to walk under. Those are the times when we need people who are willing to lend their umbrellas to a wet stranger on a rainy day. I think I'll go for a walk with my umbrella.

Sun-Young Park

She opened the letter as she strolled up the driveway from the mailbox. As she finished the first paragraph she stopped in her tracks, unable to focus because of the tears in her eyes. After a few seconds, she lifted her head toward the perfect sky and, for a brief, wonderful moment, she could hear her son singing his favorite song.

In the house, she put the mail down and called her husband at the store where he worked to tell him what had just arrived. At first, he was speechless, trying awkwardly to collect his emotions and having some difficulty.

"Read it to me," the husband said.

She spoke softly and slowly, savoring each word. When she finished, neither said anything for a long time until, finally, the husband declared: "There really is a God."

Eighteen months ago, they were living at Children's Hospital in Boston. Their nine-year-old son had been diagnosed with cancer. As if that weren't enough, the father had just been laid off by a high-tech company that was surviving only by "downsizing," a 1990s word for unemployment. Like many people affected by such management decisions, the layoff was an economic death sentence to the household. His wife was a library clerk. In addition to their son, there were three other children, girls ages seven, five and two.

Cancer is the most vicious of diseases, consuming the cells of a victim's body without discrimination. It has no conscience either, striking the very young and the very innocent as well as those much older who at least have managed to see and taste a larger slice of life.

Day after day, both parents took turns at the hospital with their sick boy. The doctors and nurses were wonderful and heroic as they managed to evoke smiles and optimism from those so wounded by the bitter reality of their illness.

Their son struck up a friendship with another boy on the floor, a 10-year-old who—like him—loved baseball. And on those dreamy summer nights when the Olde Towne Team was home, the two of them sat by a window on an upper floor in a hospital ward and listened to games on the radio as they looked at the lights of the ballpark off in the distance, washing across the July sky like some brilliant Milky Way all their own.

These two sick children became thick as thieves, joined by their passion for the Red Sox along with the anchor of their cancer. Naturally, their parents became friends, too.

The other boy was from Connecticut. His parents were

trust-fund wealthy, but even their affluence could not insulate them from the cargo of grief that attaches itself to anyone with a wounded child.

So, this boy's mother and father were deeply touched when the parents of the nine-year-old presented both boys with Red Sox jackets and two baseballs signed by Mo Vaughn.

We are a land of baseball and miracles and progress, but none of it can impede the nearly inevitable curse of cancer. And so it was that the nine-year-old died on a clear, crisp fall day when his favorite game had long fallen silent from a strike. The combination of hospitalization and unemployment had nearly bankrupted the family, yet they had to fight on for their three surviving children.

But every day was like carrying a load of bricks up some steep, never-ending hill. The only job the father found was at a variety store while his wife simply could not return to work. And on the morning she stopped in her tracks, letter in hand, their home was on the verge of foreclosure as she read that first paragraph.

> *We will never forget the kindness you showed our son at Children's. God moves in mysterious ways. We are so fortunate. Our son is doing well. We heard about your difficulty from a nurse and want you to accept what we have sent. Your son gave a lot to our son. We think about him every day and we still hear his beautiful voice singing his favorite song, "The Star Spangled Banner," when we watch the Red Sox. You gave to us. Now it is time for our family to give in return. May God bless you.*

They had enclosed $10,000. It is the kind of generous gesture, one wounded couple to another, forged forever at the edge of a gentle sadness.

Mike Barnicle

Hope in a Bottle

They say a person needs just these things to be truly happy in this world: someone to love, something to do, and something to hope for.

Tom Bodett

I truly believe everyone in their lifetime comes face-to-face with a bit of magic. It's the kind of magic that reminds you of one single word that can be easily forgotten—hope.

One blustery 1992 day as I walked along the shoreline, I watched waves roll in from a spate of thunderstorms. Trash lined the shore, along with large mounds of seaweed.

I don't know what made it catch my eye. But atop those smelly mounds, a large Canadian Club bottle was perched upright. Inside, I spotted a piece of paper—a damp slip curled with lettering on it. I clutched the bottle under my arm and got the message out. It said: Return to E. L. Cannon, Hollywood, Florida, with a note and your address and receive $20.00 U.S.

I wrote to one E. L. Cannon and learned that he and his wife had tossed the bottle from a cruise ship about 100 miles off Los Angeles after coming up from the Panama

Canal. Soon my husband, Jim and I became pen pals with Ed and Mary, who turned out to be delightful, retired world travelers who regularly cruised the planet. To this day, although they are in their 80s, I still have images of them dancing across the ship's deck.

We began exchanging short letters. During this time, I read a magazine article and grew intrigued by the country of Belize. I dreamed about its lush tropical jungles, its jaguars, its hundreds of palm-lined cays—islands—peppered inside the second longest barrier reef in the world. I liked that some of the country's descendants had come from a line of British and Scottish pirates, who once hid among the cays that laced the aqua-green Caribbean. I shared my dream with Jim, and we decided to go the next year. We collected information and saved money. On a lark, I wrote the Cannons and asked if they'd been there.

In response, a huge envelope arrived and out fell a pile of photos: Mary and Ed standing on a pier in San Pedro, Ambergris Cay, the largest island. Mary posing proudly with their fishing guide, Luz, who was holding up a giant barracuda. The Cannons had been visiting San Pedro three times a year for more than *two decades*. This seemed so ironic that we agreed Belize would be the perfect place to meet. We planned our trip for February, and decided to meet at the only hotel where the Cannons stayed because its Mayan owner Celi was like a daughter.

Meeting absolute strangers in this way seemed remarkable, but that's only the beginning. In late March, I drove home from my reporting job when I noticed a cloud fogging my right eye. I lost about 25 percent of my vision. By week's end, I was totally blind in that eye. My vision returned in a few days, but in mid-June, after some tests, the doctors delivered the news that I had multiple sclerosis. This neurological disease is unpredictable and affects each individual so differently, anything could happen—

from tingling to numbness, from blindness to total paralysis. No person reacts the same way to MS, an illness that's like a short-circuit to the brain.

I went into a tailspin—became angry, depressed and moody. I was exhausted every day. I dragged myself to work and quit writing the Cannons. I decided not to go to Belize. We hadn't saved enough money, anyway. Four months went by, and finally, I responded to some of the Cannons' letters. I told them about the multiple sclerosis and that we wouldn't join them after all.

Then came a cold and unforgettable November night. When I came home, I smelled the familiar aroma of garlic and vegetables, and Jim was cooking. I was feeling pretty miserable when I spotted a yellow envelope on the table. Jim looked up from the stove with a large smile and said: "Read it."

> *Dear Diana and Jim:*
>
> *We received your letter the day we left for Florida and we were very sorry to hear about your illness. . . . It so happens we have a niece who has a travel agency in a suburb of Cleveland, and she has arranged for two round-trip tickets from Los Angeles to San Pedro (Ambergris Cay, Belize) for you. They will be free—no charge—and will be just the medicine you need: a week or so in San Pedro, Belize.*
>
> *Congratulations! You have won the San Pedro lotto!*

I looked at my husband. "Let's go!" he shouted happily. But somehow, I just couldn't accept such a gesture. I was raised to give, not take. We agreed I would talk to my father because we were close and he always gave good advice. The prospect of talking to him, however, made us cringe. We knew the trip was doomed. My father was a man who loved to give to people, but whose pride wouldn't allow him to accept such an offer.

But my father said, "The Cannons wanted to do this or they would never have offered. You should go and consider it one of the greatest gifts anybody has ever given you." I was stunned. What he said was so true. This was a gift—a gift of hope.

And it became one that I would cling to and remember for the rest of my life. Two months before our trip, five days before Christmas, my father died. It was two days after the last time I saw him, and again, I was swallowed by a deep depression. The only thing I had left in my life, I believed, was the gift.

When we arrived in the sandy streets of San Pedro, we met the Cannons on the hotel porch they call "Happy Corner." Eddie and I listened to the waves as they roared over the reef. I talked about my father, and he talked about his. I was in the right place for healing—surrounded by an emerald sea where I would snorkel for the first time in my life and see the ocean's underwater treasures: deep caverns, fish of brilliant colors, seahorses and schools of squid.

Eddie told me something he lived by: "In this life, always give yourself something to look forward to."

And I have been doing that ever since. In 1995, we returned to the island for a reunion with the Cannons. We shared the bottle story with other tourists who came to "Happy Corner" and toasted the Cannons.

When we arrived home, we received letters from everyone we met. They all wanted to remember the bottle story. I can't thank the Cannons enough.

Their message in a bottle had returned my hope. And still does to this day.

Diana L. Chapman

The Code of the Road

Blessed are those that can give without remembering and take without forgetting.

Elizabeth Bibesco

As the daughter of a truck driver and a secretary, I grew up knowing my mother far better than my father. As a young child I was "Daddy's little girl," but then I hit those teen years and my relationship with my father no longer existed. He had spent most of my life on the road, leaving before 4:00 A.M. and arriving home well after my bedtime. By the time I was old enough to stay up past 9:00 P.M., I was no longer Daddy's little girl, I was a teenager. Now we were strangers—I didn't know him and he couldn't have known me. It was almost as if one day he went out on the truck, and, when he returned, I was 13. It took me years to understand that he had no idea what to do with me. He didn't know how to handle a teenage girl with crazed hormones and a big mouth. The little girl who adored her daddy was replaced by a horrendous teen who liked nothing better than to have the last word in every argument. And so began a lesson I will never forget . . .

I was a rebellious teenager with big dreams and an open mind. During the hardest parts of my life, I believe my mother sustained me. When she attempted to guide me, of course I fought every inch of the way. But she never let go—she held on for dear life, and finally I outgrew those raging hormones and outrageous behaviors. It was during this time that I learned an important lesson from my father. A lesson of strength, love, honesty and kindness.

One evening he returned from another day on the truck, probably delivering cargo to Brooklyn, the Bronx, Harlem or Philadelphia. He told us how that afternoon he was on the highway and saw a woman opening her trunk to take out a spare tire. He stopped, introduced himself and proceeded to take over the task of changing the blown-out tire. While he jacked up the car, the woman told him how grateful she was for his kindness. She said people's fear of crime in urban areas often dissuade local people from stopping to help one another. When Dad finished changing the tire and returning all of the equipment to the trunk of her car, she offered him a $20 bill for his help. He smiled at her and said, "No need. I have a wife and a daughter who just started driving, and my only hope is that if ever one of them breaks down on the side of the road, someone honest and friendly will stop and do for them what I just did for you." He said good-bye and headed back to the 18-wheeler he had left with its motor running on the shoulder of the road.

This was a side of my father I didn't see often. Instead, throughout my life, my Brooklyn-Italian father nonchalantly taught me the rules of the road and life through loud funny stories shared boisterously with his trucking buddies at family parties. Through the laughter, I heard explanations of "on the road" safe places to sleep, where to eat, definitions of respect, honesty and hard work, and "blue collar" survival. I was 24 years old before I realized how much I had really learned from him.

In 1992, I moved from my parents' New Jersey home to an apartment in eastern Kansas, where I worked as a volunteer for a civil rights organization. During those three and a half years I traveled almost continuously. One day, the 12-year-old daughter of a friend suggested we head to western Kansas to join the "Walk Across America for Mother Earth." As a firm believer in recycling and saving our environment, I agreed. The next day I borrowed my roommate's car for the four-hour trip.

We were almost halfway there when the left rear tire blew out. I maintained control of the car and pulled off of I-70 onto the shoulder of the road. Quite shook up, I took a deep breath and got out of the car. I went into the trunk for the spare tire. As I was removing the jack, an 18-wheeler went flying past us at top speed. I was positioning the jack when I heard the screeching of air brakes across the road. I looked up to see a trucker running across four lanes of interstate to our aid. The trucker explained that the driver of the previous 18-wheeler radioed ahead informing him that we were in trouble. He introduced himself, asked where we were going and took the jack from my hands. Within 20 minutes, the tire was changed and the jack was placed back in the trunk.

I was instructed by the driver to stop at the first auto plaza for a new tire. He explained that the spare "donut" could not make that round-trip. As we said our good-byes, I reached into my pocket and offered him a $20 bill for his help. He smiled and said in his Midwestern accent, "I have a daughter just about the same age as you—the only thanks I need is to hope that if she ever breaks down on the road, someone honest would stop to help her as I've done with you." I heard my own father's Brooklyn dialect repeating almost the same sentiment. I told the driver about my father and his experience in New Jersey. The truck driver smiled, and as he crossed the interstate, he turned and said, "Your daddy's a good man . . . he knows the *code of the road*."

I stopped at the next auto plaza to replace the tire. Using my calling card, I then dialed my parents' number, knowing everyone would be at work. I left a message for my father telling him about the truck driver who helped me and thanking Dad for knowing the code of the road.

Special thanks from a trucker's little girl to all of the drivers who know and understand the code of the road . . . especially the two gentlemen in Kansas who helped me!

Michele H. Vignola

3

ON PARENTS AND PARENTING

Making the decision to have a child—it's momentous. It is to decide forever to have your heart go walking around outside your body.

Elizabeth Stone

Cookies, Forgotten
and Forgiven

As I sat perched in the second-floor window of our brick schoolhouse that afternoon, my heart began to sink further with each passing car. This was a day I'd looked forward to for weeks: Miss Pace's fourth-grade, end-of-the-year party. Miss Pace had kept a running countdown on the blackboard all that week, and our class of nine-year-olds had bordered on insurrection by the time the much-anticipated "party Friday" had arrived.

I had happily volunteered my mother when Miss Pace requested cookie volunteers. Mom's chocolate chips reigned supreme on our block, and I knew they'd be a hit with my classmates. But two o'clock passed, and there was no sign of her. Most of the other mothers had already come and gone, dropping off their offerings of punch and crackers, chips, cupcakes and brownies. My mother was missing in action.

"Don't worry, Robbie, she'll be along soon," Miss Pace said as I gazed forlornly down at the street. I looked at the wall clock just in time to see its black minute hand shift to half-past.

Around me, the noisy party raged on, but I wouldn't budge from my window watch post. Miss Pace did her best to coax me away, but I stayed put, holding out hope that the familiar family car would round the corner, carrying my rightfully embarrassed mother with a tin of her famous cookies tucked under her arm.

The three o'clock bell soon jolted me from my thoughts and I dejectedly grabbed my book bag from my desk and shuffled out the door for home.

On the four-block walk to our house, I plotted my revenge. I would slam the front door upon entering, refuse to return her hug when she rushed over to me, and vow never to speak to her again.

The house was empty when I arrived and I looked for a note on the refrigerator that might explain my mother's absence, but found none. My chin quivered with a mixture of heartbreak and rage. For the first time in my life, my mother had let me down.

I was lying face-down on my bed upstairs when I heard her come through the front door.

"Robbie," she called out a bit urgently. "Where are you?"

I could then hear her darting frantically from room to room, wondering where I could be. I remained silent. In a moment, she mounted the steps—the sounds of her footsteps quickening as she ascended the staircase.

When she entered my room and sat beside me on my bed, I didn't move but instead stared blankly into my pillow refusing to acknowledge her presence.

"I'm so sorry, honey," she said. "I just forgot. I got busy and forgot—plain and simple."

I still didn't move. "Don't forgive her," I told myself. "She humiliated you. She forgot you. Make her pay."

Then my mother did something completely unexpected. She began to laugh. I could feel her shudder as the laughter shook her. It began quietly at first and then increased in its velocity and volume.

I was incredulous. How could she laugh at a time like this? I rolled over and faced her, ready to let her see the rage and disappointment in my eyes.

But my mother wasn't laughing at all. She was crying. "I'm so sorry," she sobbed softly. "I let you down. I let my little boy down."

She sank down on the bed and began to weep like a little girl. I was dumbstruck. I had never seen my mother cry. To my understanding, mothers weren't supposed to. I wondered if this was how I looked to her when I cried.

I desperately tried to recall her own soothing words from times past when I'd skinned knees or stubbed toes, times when she knew just the right thing to say. But in that moment of tearful plight, words of profundity abandoned me like a worn-out shoe.

"It's okay, Mom," I stammered as I reached out and gently stroked her hair. "We didn't even need those cookies. There was plenty of stuff to eat. Don't cry. It's all right. Really."

My words, as inadequate as they sounded to me, prompted my mother to sit up. She wiped her eyes, and a slight smile began to crease her tear-stained cheeks. I smiled back awkwardly, and she pulled me to her.

We didn't say another word. We just held each other in a long, silent embrace. When we came to the point where I would usually pull away, I decided that, this time, I could hold on, perhaps, just a little bit longer.

Robert Tate Miller

What's in a Name?

He who raises a child is to be called its father, not the man who only gave it birth.

Midrash, Exodus Rabbah, 46:5

I was 11 when Mom remarried. When I was four or five, she and my father had divorced. We'd gone from a bright and cheery ground-floor apartment in a safe, middle-class neighborhood, to a fourth floor, cramped and darker apartment in a poorer area of New York City. My brother and I often felt lonely and frightened, listening to police and ambulance sirens piercing the night.

In the six years we lived there, I remember envying those friends who had fathers. It was my dream to get a father for myself. My own father had completely left my life—his whereabouts a mystery. I thought that, if I had a father, he would be a powerful guardian who would magically defend me against the many perils I felt that I faced in the streets. Somehow, in that childhood fantasy, my new father would not have to work. He'd just be there for me, whenever I needed him. If other boys menaced me, Super Dad would appear and chase them off. It was pure wish fulfillment, but nonetheless a powerful dream for a frightened little boy.

Suddenly, Frank McCarty appeared in our lives. He was exciting and interesting because he was a New York City police captain of detectives. He had a gold police shield and there was a gun in a holster on his belt, under his suit coat. I don't remember the day he first appeared, but I do remember the general time and its feeling of excitement and drama. Police were the stuff of movies. Police weren't people you actually knew. I told all my friends about him. Their eyes widened as I described his gun and the stories that he told me about capturing some bad guys.

He didn't like to tell these stories, but my mom wanted him to be accepted by her sons and she knew what kids liked to hear. She'd cue him to tell a certain story and he'd acquiesce and patiently tell the story. As he got more deeply into the story, he became animated and the story took on mythic proportions.

One day, Mom asked me how I would feel if she married Frank. By this time, I was really hooked. He had taken me to the Giants game at the Polo Grounds. He had taken me to Coney Island. He talked with me. He gave me advice on how to fight back when confronted with bullies in the street. His gun gleamed darkly from under his coat. I could have a dad, a protector, someone to take me to the game. "Wow!" I said, "I'd love it!"

The date came. We went to a rural resort hotel whose owner was a friend of my mother's. Another friend of Mom's, a judge, presided over the wedding. I had a dad. Everything was going to be all right now.

I didn't know, as a child of 11, how profoundly my life would change with that one moment.

A bachelor until that point, my new dad had very limited experience with children. He didn't have the opportunity to learn his new parenting job in the natural, step-by-step way that fathers usually do. He never held a baby of his own, shared in the delight of that baby's first steps, or had to take turns feeding that child, dressing him, changing diapers, or any of the countless tasks that parenting means.

He was suddenly thrust into the role of parent, and he retreated to what he knew. His experience with kids had been limited to arresting some. His memories of parenting were of his own father's turn-of-the-century methods. He assumed that he could sit at the head of the table and issue orders that complaisant children would instantly obey.

Unfortunately for him, my mother raised us to be more independent, more participatory in dinner table discussions. We were encouraged to have opinions. She taught us to speak up as well as to listen. We weren't taught to be impolite or rude, but we were contentious.

Complicating all of this was the onset of puberty. Frank McCarty became a father, with his need to be in control, all-knowing, the leader—at the very moment that I was becoming a teen and was in the throes of the adolescent search for independence and self-authority. I was so attracted to him, I almost instantly loved him. Yet, at the same time, I was angry at him almost constantly. He stood in my way. He wasn't easy to manipulate. My brother and I could masterfully manipulate our mother. Frank McCarty was immune to our tricks.

Thus began eight years of pure hell for me and for my new dad. He announced rules and I tried to flout them. He sent me to my room for rudeness or for my attitude. I complained bitterly to my mother about his dictatorial practices. She tried hard to be the peacemaker but to no avail.

I must admit that there were many occasions in my life from age 13 until I was 20 that I was stuck in a state of anger and frustration at some perceived slight by my father. Passionate as these times were, they were punctuated by great moments with him. Going shopping with him, every week, for flowers to "surprise your mother," he'd say. Going to a ball game. Sitting in a car with him, late at night, watching a house. He'd take me on a surveillance, when he became a private detective back in New York City, if the case was an insurance fraud or something similarly non-violent. We'd sit there in the darkened car, sipping coffee, and he'd talk about "the job," as he called his career in the police department. I felt so special, so loved, so included at these times. This was exactly what my fantasy had been. A dad who loved me, who'd do things with me.

I remember many, many nights, sitting in front of him on an ottoman and he'd rub my back as we watched TV together. He gave great hugs. He wasn't afraid to say, "I love you." I found the tenderness this rough-and-ready guy was able to express remarkable. However, he could go from these intimate moments to red-faced yelling and sputtering anger if I did or said something that he thought was rude. His temper was a natural phenomenon akin to a tornado. It was a fearsome thing to watch and it was even scarier to be the target of it.

In high school, the angry moments increased and my closeness with him decreased. By the time I was in college, I was mostly alienated from him. I got a lot of mileage in terms of sympathy from my friends, if I put him down in my conversations with them. I'd tell stories of his latest "atrocity," and stuck in adolescence just as I was, they'd murmur sympathetically about how much we all had to put up with from our dads.

It was my last year in college. I don't know if there was any one event that precipitated it other than my getting a year older and going further along on the road to maturity, but I started rethinking my relationship with him.

I thought, "Here's a guy who falls in love with my mother and he's stuck with two teenage boys as the price of being married to her. He didn't fall in love with two kids, just my mother. But we came with the package.

"And look what he does: He doesn't just relate to her and ignore us. No, he tries his very hardest to be a real father to me. He risks the relationship all the time. He tried to teach me a set of values. He made me do my homework. He took me to the emergency room at two in the morning. He paid for my education without a grumble. He taught me how to tie a tie. He did all the daddy things without thought of payback. That's really something. I guess I'm a lucky kid to have him in my life."

I knew that my dad had come from an old New England Irish family. They were never famous, powerful or wealthy, but they had been here a long, long time. He felt sad that he was the last to "carry the name." "It'll die with me," he said. His brother had died without children and his sisters, having married and taken their husbands' names, wouldn't carry on that name either.

My brother and I still carried the name of our biological father; the man who sired me, but didn't stay around for the rest of the job. The thought troubled me that the man who really was my father, as I understood that word, would not be celebrated by having a son with his own name.

Ideas occur to us and gradually coalesce into behavior. The idea got stronger and stronger. My thoughts were increasingly taken over by this idea. Finally, action was inevitable. I went to an attorney and then to a court. Secretly, I had my name changed to McCarty. I told no one. I waited three months until my dad's birthday in October.

He opened the birthday card slowly. Usually when I gave him a card, it was attached to a box with his gift. This time there was no box, just the envelope. He pulled out the card and, with it, a certificate from a court.

I wrote on the card, "No store sells true gifts for father and son. You gave me roots, I give you branches."

It was one of only two or three times I ever saw my dad cry. Tears came unbidden to his eyes. He smiled and shook his head and sighed. Then he got up and enfolded me in one of his famous bear hugs. "Thank you, boy, thank you. I just don't know what to say. Thank you." My mom was stunned, too. And very happy for both of us. The war was over. I'd brought the armistice agreement, wrapped in a birthday card.

Hanoch McCarty

The Only Memory That Lingers

You never know when you're making a memory.

Rickie Lee Jones

I have many memories about my father and about growing up with him in our apartment next to the elevated train tracks. For 20 years, we listened to the roar of the train as it passed by his bedroom window. Late at night, he waited alone on the tracks for the train that took him to his job at a factory, where he worked the midnight shift.

On this particular night, I waited with him in the dark to say good-bye. His face was grim. His youngest son had been drafted. I would be sworn in at six the next morning, while he stood at his paper-cutting machine in the factory.

My father had talked about his anger. He didn't want *them* to take his child, only 19 years old, who had never had a drink or smoked a cigarette, to fight a war in Europe. He placed his hands on my slim shoulders. "You be careful, Srulic, and if you ever need anything, write to me and I'll see that you get it."

Suddenly, he heard the roar of the approaching train. He held me tightly in his arms and gently kissed me on the cheek. With tear-filled eyes, he murmured, "I love you, my son." Then the train arrived, the doors closed him inside, and he disappeared into the night.

One month later, at age 46, my father died. I am 76 as I sit and write this. I once heard Pete Hamill, the New York reporter, say that memories are man's greatest inheritance, and I have to agree. I've lived through four invasions in World War II. I've had a life full of all kinds of experiences. But the only memory that lingers is of the night when my dad said, "I love you, my son."

Ted Kruger

Urbana Farewell

*Your children are always your babies, even if
they have gray hair.*

Janet Leigh

In 15 minutes, a bus is due to arrive at the station to
take me back home to Bozeman, Montana. In 15 minutes,
my life will turn a corner and my relationship with my
youngest son, Keith, will alter.

We drove to Urbana together after Christmas to get him
set up in an apartment and a new life. He will attend the
University of Illinois on a scholarship to play wheelchair
basketball. Keith is a paraplegic.

"Well, Mom, I guess this is it. No more 'stretchy sing
pow.'" Keith speaks in a family code. That is his way of saying: "I won't have anyone to stretch my legs in the morning" implying he'll have to do other things for himself, too,
like dishes and laundry. It's also his way of acknowledging
all the little things we share, like the code itself.

"No more 'techy sing pow,'" I reply. That means, "You
won't be able to razz me about the inept way I handle the
physical world." (A "tech" is our family slang for someone,

like me, who is allergic to the techno gadgetry of our times.)
My "techniness" exasperates him. But it delights him, too,
because he never tires of wise-cracking at my expense. To
him, I am the "Dorisaurus," a creature bound for extinction.
I must agree, I am an analog woman in a digital world. Our
affectionate estrangement is a pattern that started early.
Even as a child, when we went shopping together, he pre-
tended he didn't know me, and walked 20 cool paces before
or behind, always glancing out the corner of his eye to keep
me in range. Our distance created an ample laughing space
we could both enjoy as we bumbled along together.

We are both very aware that our mutually endearing
relationship is changing. Fortunately, as a result of the
forced intimacy between "caregiver and client," I learned
to banter easily with my son. Many mothers would find
the lightheartedness in our relationship remarkable. But
for the accident, I would probably be lucky to have three
of four stiff phone calls a year from Keith—that's the way
things were going.

Neither of us looks at the other, in fact we both gladly
stare anywhere else. We are aware of others in the bus station. I conclude that the traveler across from me only pre-
tends to read his gold-embossed supermarket novel. That
way, he can keep a polite distance from what is obviously
a private and touching moment. On the other hand, I
doubt that the other passengers—a head between earphones and a mouth devouring a mound of deli ribs—
notice anything whatsoever beyond a radius of six inches.
Still they figure in as an obligatory audience.

I want to have the parting moment behind us, so I move
to hasten it. "No use for you to wait here, Keith. It will be
half an hour before we're ready to board. I'll be fine."

Keith receives my suggestion with relief. "Okay, then."

Frankly, I had hoped for a polite protest, one I could
overcome with a slightly martyrish, "No, really. I'll be

fine." But protestations and games of manners are not Keith's style. He prepares to leave.

Now comes the inevitable part. I bend down to hug my son for what could turn out to be the last time for a long while. Unfortunately, I don't remember that the only way to hug someone gracefully in a wheelchair is to kneel, and so our embrace feels awkward. We deliver the standard three pats which in our family signifies "It is finished," or "Go with God," or in this case, "Free to go."

For an instant our eyes meet. His eyes are red, but he is not crying. Instead, he laughs nervously. He is officially "on his own" for the first time in his life.

Undoubtedly, Keith would have been independent at 18 were it not for that last surfing safari with Richard, his best friend. They headed up Pacific Coast Highway early one morning in July 1989. Richard, who had only been driving for a few months, sat behind the wheel of my Nissan pickup. Out late the night before, Keith dozed in the passenger seat. Richard took a curve too fast and too wide. The truck spun out on the gravel shoulder and rolled several times. Neither of them lost consciousness, but Keith was pinned in the crushed cab. Realizing they were both alive, Richard joked, "Hey, man! Are you there?"

"Half of me is. I can't be sure about the rest," was Keith's fateful reply. Within the hour, the "jaws of life" arrived and pried Keith out. A helicopter lifted him to one of the best equipped trauma centers in the world. Richard escaped with minor injuries. Keith turned 17 the next day in Northridge Hospital.

The supermarket novel man glances up. Does he see a woman whose last child is leaving her care; a young man going forth in the time-honored way to seek his fortune? I wonder what he sees.

Keith pivots on his racing wheels and heads out

smartly, self-consciously, with determination in each stroke. I watch him out the window. When he gets to the car, he swings his body gracefully into the driver's seat and deftly disassembles the chair. Keith is not a "tech," no wasted motion. Feeling my eyes on him, he looks up. I wave; he waves back.

That is the signal for the tears I have been holding back. I wonder if Keith is crying, too. "Not like him," I decide, "but still, not beyond him." I know it's a good thing that there are mysterious depths in my children that I need not fathom.

I am suddenly aware of curious eyes behind me. The novel, the earphones and the ribs have lost their appeal. Attention is focused on me. It registers as compassion.

Keith drives by the front door of the station and signals again. But this time it is not a wave, it is a salute.

Doris W. Davis

For Better or For Worse®   by Lynn Johnston

My Own Experience

No external advantages can supply self-reliance. The force of one's being . . . must come from within.

R. W. Clark

My first awareness of her was her hands. I don't remember how old I was, but my whole being and existence were associated with those hands. Those hands belonged to my mom, and she is blind.

I can remember sitting at the kitchen table coloring a picture. "Look at my picture, Mom. It's all finished."

"Oh, that's pretty," she replied, and kept right on doing whatever she was doing.

"No, look at my picture with your fingers," I insisted. She then came to me, and I ran her hand all over the picture. I always enjoyed her excited response that the picture was lovely.

It never occurred to me that it was strange how she felt things with her hands, how she touched my face or things I showed her. I did realize that my dad looked at me and at the things I showed to him with his eyes, and so did Grandma or any other person who came into our house; but I never thought it unusual that Mom didn't use her eyes.

I can still remember how she combed my long hair. She put the thumb of her left hand between my eyebrows, just at the top of my nose, and her forefinger at the crown of my head. She was probably lining up those two points, and then she'd bring the comb from her forefinger down to meet the thumb. Thus, she hoped the part would be down the middle of my head. I never questioned her ability to do this task.

When I fell down many times at play, came in crying and told Mom that my knee was bleeding, her gentle hands washed my knee and skillfully applied a bandage.

One day I found out, unfortunately, that there were certain things my mother wouldn't touch. I found a tiny dead bird lying on the sidewalk in front of our house and brought it into the house to show Mom. "Look what I found," I said, as I took her hand to touch the bird. "What is it?" she asked. She lightly touched the dead creature in my outstretched palm, and I could hear the terror in her voice as she asked once more, "What is that?"

"A little dead bird," I answered. She screamed then and quickly drew back her hand and ordered me and the bird outside and admonished me never to let her touch such a thing again.

I could never quite reckon with her powers of smell, hearing and touch. One day, I saw a plate of cookies that Mom had just placed on the table. I slyly took one and looked at her to see what she would say. She didn't say a word and, of course, I thought as long as she didn't feel with those hands what I'd done, she didn't know. I didn't realize that she could hear me chew. Just as I passed by her munching my cookie, she caught my arm. "Next time,

Karrey, please ask me for that cookie instead of taking it," she said. "You can have all you want, just ask next time."

I have an older brother and sister and a younger brother, and none of us could quite figure out how she knew which one of us did a certain thing. One day my older brother brought a stray dog into the house and sneaked him up the stairs into his bedroom. In a short while my mom marched up the stairs, opened his bedroom door, and ordered the dog to be put outside. We were amazed she figured out there was a dog in the house.

As I grew older, I realized that Mom reared us psychologically. And with those sharp ears and nose of hers, she put two and two together and usually came up with the right answer. She had heard the dog's toenails clicking on the bedroom floor.

And that nose of hers. How it knew so much! One day my friend and I were playing with dolls in my bedroom. I slipped into Mom's room and doused the dolls with some of her perfume. Then I made the mistake of running downstairs to ask Mom a question. She immediately told me that she knew I had been in her bedroom and used her perfume.

Those ears. How they knew the things we did. I was all alone in the living room one night doing my homework with the TV running softly. Mom walked into the room and asked, "Karrey, are you doing your homework or watching TV?" I was slightly surprised but answered her and went on with my homework. Later I thought about it and wondered how she knew that I was the one in the living room and not one of my brothers or sisters. I asked her. "Sorry, honey," she said patting my head. "Even though your adenoids are gone, you still breathe through your mouth. I heard you."

Mom had a good sense of direction, too. She had a tandem bicycle and we took turns riding with her. I sat on the front seat and steered and pedaled and she sat on the back seat. She always seemed to know where we were and called out directions loud and clear. She always knew when we were approaching an intersection or when a fast-moving car was coming up on the right side.

How did she know that while I was taking a bath one night, when I was about nine years old, that I hadn't washed any part of myself? I was busy playing with the toys in the water and having a great time. "Karrey, you haven't touched your face or ears or anything, have you?" I hadn't, but how did she know? Of course she knew that a little girl playing with toys in a bathtub would not stop to wash. I realized that she also used her mind's eye in rearing us.

The one thing, however, that used to concern us was the fact that Mom never really knew what we looked like. One day when I was about 17 and standing in front of the bathroom mirror combing my hair, I asked, "You really don't know what any of us look like, do you, Mom?" She was feeling my hair to see how long it was.

"Of course I do," she answered.

"I know what you looked like the day they laid your tiny little body in my arms for the first time. I felt every inch of you and felt the soft fuzz on your head. I knew that you were blond because your daddy told me so. I knew that your eyes were blue because they told me so. I know that you are very pretty because people tell me you are. But I really know what you are like—what you are like inside." My eyes grew misty.

"I know that you're lithe and strong because you love being on the tennis court. I know that you have a good nature because I hear you talk to the cat and to small children. I know you are tender-hearted. I know you are vulnerable because I've seen your hurt reactions to someone's remarks. I know that you have character because you have the courage to stand up and defend your convictions. I know that you have a respect for human beings because of the way you treat me. I know that you have wisdom because you conduct yourself wisely for a girl your age. I also know that you have a will of your own because I've seen a hint of temper, which tells me that no one can dissuade you from doing the right things. I know that you have family devotion because I've heard you defending your brothers and sister. I know that you possess a great capacity for love because you've shown it to me and to your father many times. You have never indicated in any way that you were short-changed because you have a blind mother. So, dear," and she drew me close to her, "I see you and I know exactly what you look like, and to me you are beautiful."

That was 10 years ago, and recently I became a mother. When they laid my precious little son in my arms, I, like my mother, was able to see my child and know how beautiful he was. The only difference was that I could see him with my eyes. But sometime I'd like to turn out the lights, hold and touch him, and see if I can feel all the things my mother felt.

Karrey Janvrin Lindenberg

For Better or For Worse® **by Lynn Johnston**

A Simple Act of Love

A thousand words will not leave so deep an impression as one deed.

Henrik Ibsen

When I was growing up, my father always stopped what he was doing and listened while I'd breathlessly fill him in on my day. For him, no subject was off-limits. When I was a lanky and awkward 13, Dad coached me on how to stand and walk like a lady. At 17 and madly in love, I sought his advice on pursuing a new student at school. "Keep the conversation neutral," he counseled. "And ask him about his car."

I followed his suggestions and gave him daily progress reports: "Terry walked me to my locker!" "Guess what? Terry held my hand!" "Dad! He asked me out!" Terry and I went steady for over a year, and soon Dad was joking, "I can tell you how to get a man; the hard part is getting rid of him."

By the time I graduated from college, I was ready to spread my wings. I got a job teaching special education at a school in Coachella, California, a desert town about 170 miles from home. It was no dream job. Low-income housing across the street from the school was a haven for drug users. Street gangs hung around the school after dark. Many of my charges, emotionally disturbed 10- to 14-year-old boys, had been arrested for shoplifting, car theft or arson.

"Be careful," Dad warned me during one of my frequent weekend visits home. He was concerned about my living alone, but I was 23, enthusiastic and naive, and I needed to be on my own. Besides, teaching jobs were tight in 1974, and I felt lucky to have one.

"Don't worry," I reassured him, as I loaded up the car to start my trip back to the desert and my job.

Several evenings later I stayed after school to rearrange my classroom. Finished, I turned out the light and closed the door. Then I headed toward the gate. It was locked! I looked around. Everyone—teachers, custodians, secretaries—had gone home and, not realizing I was still there, stranded me on the school grounds. I glanced at my watch—it was almost 6 P.M. I had been so engrossed in my work that I hadn't noticed the time.

After checking all the exits, I found just enough room to squeeze under a gate in the rear of the school. I pushed my purse through first, lay on my back and slowly edged through.

I retrieved my purse and walked toward my car, parked in a field behind the building. Eerie shadows fell across the schoolyard.

Suddenly, I heard voices. I glanced around and saw at least eight high-school-age boys following me. They were half a block away. Even in the near darkness I could see they were wearing gang insignia.

"Hey!" one called out. "You a teacher?"

"Nah, she's too young—must be an aide!" another said.

As I walked faster, they continued taunting me. "Hey! She's kinda cute!"

Quickening my pace, I reached into my shoulder bag to get my key ring. *If I have the keys in my hands,* I thought, *I can unlock the car and get in before . . .* My heart was pounding.

Frantically, I felt all over the inside of my handbag. But the key ring wasn't there!

"Hey! Let's get the lady!" one boy shouted.

Dear Lord, please help me, I prayed silently. Suddenly, my fingers wrapped around a loose key in my purse. I didn't even know if it was for my car, but I took it out and clutched it firmly.

I jogged across the grass to my car and tried the key. It worked! I opened the door, slid in and locked it—just as the teenagers surrounded the car, kicking the sides and banging on the roof. Trembling, I started the engine and drove away.

Later, some teachers went back to the school with me. With flashlights, we found the key ring on the ground by the gate, where it had fallen as I slid through.

When I returned to my apartment, the phone was ringing. It was Dad. I didn't tell him about my ordeal; I didn't want to worry him.

"Oh, I forgot to tell you!" he said. "I had an extra car key made and slipped it into your pocketbook—just in case you ever need it."

Today, I keep that key in my dresser drawer and treasure it. Whenever I hold it in my hand, I am reminded of all the wonderful things Dad has done for me over the years. I realize that, although he is now 68 and I am 40, I still look to him for wisdom, guidance and reassurance. Most of all, I marvel at the fact that his thoughtful gesture of making the extra key may have saved my life. And I understand how a simple act of love can make extraordinary things happen.

Sharon Whitley
Appeared in Reader's Digest, 1992

Permission to Cry

Treasure the love you receive above all. It will survive long after your gold and good health have vanished.

Og Mandino

Alone in the wheel of light at the dining room table, surrounded by an otherwise darkened house, I sat in tears.

Finally, I'd succeeded in getting both kids to bed. A relatively new single parent, I had to be both Mommy and Daddy to my two little children. I got them both washed, accompanied by shrieks of delight, crazy running around, laughing and throwing things. More or less calmed down, they lay in their beds as I gave each the prescribed five minutes of back rubs. Then I took up my guitar and began the nighttime ritual of folk songs, ending with "All the Pretty Little Horses," both kids' favorite. I sang it over and over, gradually reducing the tempo and the volume until they seemed fully engaged in sleep.

A recently divorced man with full custody of his children, I was determined to give them as normal and stable a home life as possible. I put on a happy face for them. I kept their activities as close to how they had always been as I could. This nightly ritual was just as it had always been with the exception that their mother was now missing. There, I had done it again: another night successfully concluded.

I had risen slowly, gingerly, trying to avoid making even the least sound which might start them up again, asking for more songs and more stories. I tiptoed out of their room, closed the door part way, and went downstairs.

Sitting at the dining room table, I slumped in my chair, aware that this was the first time since I came home from work that I'd been able to just sit down. I had cooked and served and encouraged two little ones to eat. I had done the dishes while responding to their many requests for attention. I helped my oldest with her second grade homework and appreciated my youngest's drawings and oohed over his elaborate construction of Lego blocks. The bath, the stories, the backrubs, the singing and now, at long last, a brief moment for myself. The silence was a relief, for the moment.

Then it all crowded in on me: the fatigue, the weight of the responsibility, the worry about bills I wasn't sure I could pay that month. The endless details of running a house. Only a short time before, I'd been married and had a partner to share these chores, these bills, these worries.

And loneliness. I felt as though I were at the bottom of a great sea of loneliness. It all came together and I was at once lost, overwhelmed. Unexpected, convulsive sobs overtook me. I sat there, silently sobbing.

Just then, a pair of little arms went around my middle and a little face peered up at me. I looked down into my five-year-old son's sympathetic face.

I was embarrassed to be seen crying by my son. "I'm sorry, Ethan, I didn't know you were still awake." I don't know why it is, but so many people apologize when they cry and I was no exception. "I didn't mean to cry. I'm sorry. I'm just a little sad tonight."

"It's okay, Daddy. It's okay to cry, *you're just a person.*"

I can't express how happy he made me, this little boy, who in the wisdom of innocence, gave me permission to cry. He seemed to be saying that I didn't have to always be strong, that it was occasionally possible to allow myself to feel weak and let out my feelings.

He crept into my lap and we hugged and talked for a while, and I took him back up to his bed and tucked him in. Somehow, it was possible for me to get to sleep that night, too. Thank you, my son.

Hanoch McCarty

The Perfect Hug

Please continue to look at your children as valuable treasures. Honor them and yourself.

Bernie Siegel

The room was filling up with teachers and administrators. It was a long room with those bare and fading painted walls that we've come to associate with schools, church rectories and other under-funded institutions. The only details to relieve the plainness were the flag up on the front wall and the cracked slate chalkboard. This huge room served many purposes: classroom, meeting space and recreation hall for this old, small college.

I had been invited to present a workshop on innovative teaching methods to a large group of local teachers.

At that moment in time, I was a single parent with full custody of my two little children. My daughter, Shayna, was about seven years old and my son, Ethan, was just five. Because this was not a school day, I had arranged for a babysitter to watch my children while I drove to the conference site. Unfortunately, the sitter canceled the morning of the conference and I had to take both children with me. They had been at many of my presentations before so they knew "the drill." They knew they had to sit and play quietly.

Shayna brought books and drawing materials to occupy her time. She also brought her doll collection including a box of Barbie dolls and their myriad accessories. Ethan brought a small suitcase of building blocks and soldier dolls with all their guns and equipment.

They sat at a table at the very back of the room, facing away from the front where I would be presenting, both fully engrossed in play.

The teachers group was lively and responsive. Every activity I proposed they enthusiastically made their own. Participation was nearly total as I demonstrated teaching methods and organized small groups to share ideas.

At one point, a teacher raised her hand and said, "I wonder what you'd suggest about hugging."

"Tell me more about your concern," I replied.

"Well, I teach elementary school—fourth- and fifth-grade combined—and sometimes I just want to hug the kids, especially the ones who are often in trouble. Do you think it's all right to do that?"

"It's a strange world, indeed, that we are living in," I replied. "Hugging is such a natural and spontaneous display of affection. It is often the very best thing you can do when a child is hurting, depressed, crying or frightened. Yet we've learned to be worried about it. There have been, sadly enough, too many cases reported in the media, of adults touching kids inappropriately. So it is important to have guidelines and clear limits to how, when and where we touch kids. Yes, I think hugging is a very good thing to do."

I concluded with this comment: "You know, when adults hug each other, there's always a bit of self-consciousness about it. Part of you is committed to the hug and part of you may be thinking something like, 'I wonder if this person understands what I really mean by this hug,' or 'I wonder what this person means by *his* or *her* hug!' or 'I wonder if anyone else is watching this hug and I wonder what they think,' or [I added for the sake of humor] even, 'I wonder if I've paid my MasterCard bill.'" The group roared with laughter.

"As adults, because we've been through so many experiences, we each bring our entire personal history into the hug and all the concerns that come with that history. Further, we are worried about, thinking about, planning for, engaged in, so many, many things that it's hard to just be in the hug totally and completely. The reason I am thinking about this is that I can see my children at the back of the room."

At this, the group turned their heads to look at my children who were still sitting quietly, engrossed in play, facing away from the group. Then the participants turned back to me as I went on.

"You see, when I get home at the end of a work day, as tired as I am, one of the things I most look forward to is a hug from my children. As young as they are, they have less history and fewer complicated worries and no bills to pay. As I walk in the door, they each almost fly up my body and hug and kiss me. My son particularly nearly melts his body into mine, burying his face in my neck and just hugs me. I believe that at such moments he is fully, completely and only hugging me, without distracting thoughts and without reservation. And it's the most tender moment in my life!" The group smiled approvingly and that started a number of side conversations that went on for several minutes before we went on with the workshop.

Six or seven weeks later I was coming home from a long and exhausting day at the university where I taught educational psychology. I pulled into the garage, took my briefcase and entered the house through the kitchen door. Both children came flying down the stairs screaming, "Daddy, Daddy, Daddy!" and Shayna leaped into my arms, "I missed you, Daddy. Do you know what I did?" And of course I wanted to know all about what she had done. Their nanny stood beaming in the background as Shayna told her story. Then, done with me, Shayna ran gaily out of the kitchen and returned to her latest project.

Ethan had barely contained himself. He, too, leaped up on my chest and hugged me with all his might. He buried his face in my neck and his breathing slowed. His body softened as he seemed to melt into me. Then he raised his head slightly away from my neck and whispered in my ear, "I wonder if I paid my MasterCard bill!"

Hanoch McCarty

HAGAR

Winners and Winners

*H*onesty *is the first chapter in the book of wisdom.*

Thomas Jefferson

As a high school coach, I did all I could to help my boys win their games. I rooted as hard for victory as they did.

A dramatic incident, however, following a game in which I officiated as a referee, changed my perspective on victories and defeats. I was refereeing a league championship basketball game in New Rochelle, New York, between New Rochelle and Yonkers High. New Rochelle was coached by Dan O'Brien, Yonkers by Les Beck.

The gym was crowded to capacity, and the volume of noise made it impossible to hear. The game was well played and closely contested. Yonkers was leading by one point as I glanced at the clock and discovered there were but 30 seconds left to play. Yonkers, in possession of the ball, passed off—shot—missed. New Rochelle recovered—pushed the ball up court—shot. The ball rolled tantalizingly around the rim and off. The fans shrieked.

New Rochelle, the home team, recovered the ball, and tapped it in for what looked like victory. The tumult was deafening. I glanced at the clock and saw that the game was over. I hadn't heard the final buzzer because of the noise. I checked with the other official, but he could not help me.

Still seeking help in this bedlam, I approached the time-keeper, a young man of 17 or so. He said, "Mr. Covino, the buzzer went off as the ball rolled off the rim, before the final tap-in was made."

I was in the unenviable position of having to tell Coach O'Brien the sad news. "Dan," I said, "time ran out before the final basket was tapped in. Yonkers won the game."

His face clouded over. The young timekeeper came up. He said, "I'm sorry, Dad. The time ran out before the final basket."

Suddenly, like the sun coming out from behind a cloud, Coach O'Brien's face lit up. He said, "That's okay, Joe. You did what you had to do. I'm proud of you."

Turning to me, he said, "Al, I want you to meet my son, Joe."

The two of them then walked off the court together, the coach's arm around his son's shoulder.

Al Covino
Submitted by Rob Nelson

PEANUTS reprinted by permission of United Feature Syndicate, Inc.

When You Thought I Wasn't Looking

When you thought I wasn't looking you hung my first painting
on the refrigerator
And I wanted to paint another.
When you thought I wasn't looking you fed a stray cat and I
thought it was good to be kind to animals
When you thought I wasn't looking you baked a birthday cake
just for me
And I knew that little things were special things.
When you thought I wasn't looking you said a prayer
And I believed there was a God that I could always talk to.
When you thought I wasn't looking you kissed me good-night
And I felt loved.
When you thought I wasn't looking I saw tears come from your
eyes
And I learned that sometimes things hurt but that it's alright
to cry.
When you thought I wasn't looking you smiled
And it made me want to look that pretty too.
When you thought I wasn't looking you cared
And I wanted to be everything I could be.
When you thought I wasn't looking I looked . . .
And wanted to say thanks for all those things you did
When you thought I wasn't looking.

Mary Rita Schilke Korzan

Lessons in Baseball

There are always two choices. Two paths to take,
one is easy. And its only reward is that it's easy.

Source Unknown

As an 11-year-old, I was addicted to baseball. I listened to baseball games on the radio. I watched them on TV. The books I read were about baseball. I took baseball cards to church in hopes of trading with other baseball card junkies. My fantasies? All about baseball.

I played baseball whenever and wherever I could. I played organized or sandlot. I played catch with my brother, with my father, with friends. If all else failed, I bounced a rubber ball off the porch stairs, imagining all kinds of wonderful things happening to me and my team.

With this attitude, I entered the 1956 Little League season. I was a shortstop. Not good, not bad. Just addicted.

Gordon was not addicted. Nor was he good. He moved into our neighborhood that year and signed up to play baseball. The kindest way to describe Gordon's baseball skills is to say that he didn't have any. He couldn't catch. He couldn't hit. He couldn't throw. He couldn't run.

In fact, Gordon was afraid of the ball.

I was relieved when the final selections were made and Gordon was assigned to another team. Everyone had to play at least half of each game, and I couldn't see Gordon improving my team's chances in any way. Too bad for the other team.

After two weeks of practice, Gordon dropped out. My friends on his team laughed when they told me how their coach directed two of the team's better players to walk Gordon into the woods and have a chat with him. "Get lost" was the message they delivered, and "get lost" was the message that was heard.

Gordon got lost.

That scenario violated my 11-year-old sense of justice, so I did what any indignant shortstop would do. I tattled. I told my coach the whole story. I shared the episode in full detail, figuring my coach would complain to the league office and have Gordon returned to his original team. Justice and my team's chances of winning would both be served.

I was wrong. My coach decided that Gordon needed to be on a team that wanted him—one that treated him with respect, one that gave everyone a fair chance to contribute according to his own ability.

Gordon joined our team.

I wish I could say Gordon got the big hit in the big game with two outs in the final inning. It didn't happen. I don't think Gordon even hit a foul ball the entire season. Baseballs hit in his direction (right field) went over him, by him, through him or off him.

It wasn't that Gordon didn't get help. The coach gave him extra batting practice and worked with him on his fielding, all without much improvement.

I'm not sure if Gordon learned anything from my coach that year. I know I did. I learned to bunt without tipping off my intention. I learned to tag up on a fly if there were less than two outs. I learned to make a smoother pivot around second base on a double play.

I learned a lot from my coach that summer, but my most important lessons weren't about baseball. They were about character and integrity. I learned that everyone has worth, whether they can hit .300 or .030. I learned that we all have value, whether we can stop the ball or have to turn and chase it. I learned that doing what is right, fair and honorable is more important than winning or losing.

It felt good to be on that team that year. I'm grateful that man was my coach. I was proud to be his shortstop and his son.

Chick Moorman

Catch of a Lifetime

The most permanent lessons in morals are those which come, not of booky teaching, but of experience.

Mark Twain

He was 11 years old and went fishing every chance he got from the dock at his family's cabin on an island in the middle of a New Hampshire lake.

On the day before the bass season opened, he and his father were fishing early in the evening, catching sunfish and perch with worms. Then he tied on a small silver lure and practiced casting. The lure struck the water and caused colored ripples in the sunset, then silver ripples as the moon rose over the lake.

When his pole doubled over, he knew something huge was on the other end. His father watched with admiration as the boy skillfully worked the fish alongside the dock.

Finally, he very gingerly lifted the exhausted fish from the water. It was the largest one he had ever seen, but it was a bass.

The boy and his father looked at the handsome fish, gills playing back and forth in the moonlight. The father lit a match and looked at his watch. It was 10 P.M.—two hours before the season opened. He looked at the fish, then at the boy.

"You'll have to put it back, Son," he said.

"Dad!" cried the boy.

"There will be other fish," said his father.

"Not as big as this one," cried the boy.

He looked around the lake. No other fishermen or boats were anywhere around in the moonlight. He looked again at his father.

Even though no one had seen them, nor could anyone ever know what time he caught the fish, the boy could tell by the clarity of his father's voice that the decision was not negotiable. He slowly worked the hook out of the lip of the huge bass and lowered it into the black water.

The creature swished its powerful body and disappeared. The boy suspected that he would never again see such a great fish.

That was 34 years ago. Today, the boy is a successful architect in New York City. His father's cabin is still there on the island in the middle of the lake. He takes his own son and daughters fishing from the same dock.

And he was right. He has never again caught such a magnificent fish as the one he landed that night long ago. But he does see that same fish—again and again—every time he comes up against a question of ethics.

For, as his father taught him, ethics are simple matters of right and wrong. It is only the practice of ethics that is difficult. Do we do right when no one is looking? Do we refuse to cut corners to get the design in on time? Or refuse to trade stocks based on information that we know we aren't supposed to have?

We would if we were taught to put the fish back when we were young. For we would have learned the truth.

The decision to do right lives fresh and fragrant in our memory. It is a story we will proudly tell our friends and grandchildren.

Not about how we had a chance to beat the system and took it, but about how we did the right thing and were forever strengthened.

James P. Lenfestey
Submitted by Diana Von Holdt

Letters to Eileen

A child needs your love most when she deserves it the least.

Anonymous

I have three children. Paul, the oldest and only boy, is named for his dad. Theresa, the baby of the family, has her daddy's brown eyes and curly hair.

Eileen is the middle child. She is named for me and my mother whose name was Eileen Ann. When I was born, my mother turned it around and named me Ann Eileen. So when my first girl was born, I did the same thing, naming her Eileen Ann.

Eileen showed a streak of independence from the early age of five months. She refused to let anyone feed her, determined to do things her way.

All three kids were great fun to be around. They worked hard, had senses of humor and did well in what they attempted. Like all homes, however, there were times when we initiated a discussion of some behavior that their dad and I wanted improved. With Paul and Theresa, the reactions ranged from quiet agreement to vocal disagreements, but always with a mutual clearing of the air.

With Eileen there were never any discussions. She immediately objected to our right to have an opinion, stomped up the stairs to her room, slammed the door, turned the music up loud and announced she did not want to discuss it! Several times in the early days I tried reasoning with her, but this only irritated her further.

One day out of a need for Eileen to hear our side, I wrote her a letter. In the letter I explained her dad's and my position and what we wanted changed. I waited until she left for school the next day to put the letter on her bed. She never mentioned the letter, and I never found any evidence of it. But her behavior changed!

As the years passed, there were more letters left while she was at school, at work or on a date—probably two or three letters a year for a period of 14 years. She never acknowledged the letters or discussed what was in them, but her behavior would change. Occasionally she stated as she went upstairs, "And don't write me one of those letters!" Of course, I wrote a letter.

Eileen's dad died in 1990. Three years later, she got engaged, and I was determined not to be the overbearing mother of the bride. Everything went well until about a month before the wedding. We had a disagreement. She indignantly told me she was 24 years old and a special education teacher about to be married. She also told me not to write her a letter! I wrote her a letter.

Three days before the wedding, Eileen was packing things to move to her new home. She told me there was a box in her closet that was not to be thrown away. "It contains all the letters you ever wrote me. Sometimes I re-read them and someday I will read them to my daughter. Thank you, Mom."

Thank you, Eileen.

Ann E. Weeks

Reprinted by permission of Hanoch McCarty.

4

ON TEACHING
AND
LEARNING

Education is not the filling of a pail, but the lighting of a fire.

William Butler Yeats

For Better or For Worse®   **by Lynn Johnston**

Nouns and Adverbs

Hope is the parent of faith!

Cyrus Augustus Bartol

Several years ago, a public school teacher was hired and assigned to visit children who were patients in a large city hospital. Her job was to tutor them with their schoolwork so they wouldn't be too far behind when well enough to return to school.

One day, this teacher received a routine call requesting that she visit a particular child. She took the boy's name, hospital and room number and was told by the teacher on the other end of the line, "We're studying nouns and adverbs in class now. I'd be grateful if you could help him with his homework so he doesn't fall behind the others."

It wasn't until the visiting teacher got outside the boy's room that she realized it was located in the hospital's burn unit. No one had prepared her for what she was about to discover on the other side of the door. Before she was allowed to enter, she had to put on a sterile hospital gown and cap because of the possibility of infection. She was told not to touch the boy or his bed. She could stand near but must speak through the mask she had to wear.

When she had finally completed all the preliminary washings and was dressed in the prescribed coverings, she took a deep breath and walked into the room. The young boy, horribly burned, was obviously in great pain. The teacher felt awkward and didn't know what to say, but she had gone too far to turn around and walk out. Finally she was able to stammer out, "I'm the special visiting hospital teacher, and your teacher sent me to help you with your nouns and adverbs." Afterward, she thought it was not one of her more successful tutoring sessions.

The next morning when she returned, one of the nurses on the burn unit asked her, "What did you do to that boy?"

Before she could finish a profusion of apologies, the nurse interrupted her by saying, "You don't understand. We've been worried about him, but ever since you were here yesterday his whole attitude has changed. He's fighting back, responding to treatment . . . it's as though he's decided to live."

The boy himself later explained that he had completely given up hope and felt he was going to die, until he saw that special teacher. Everything had changed with an insight gained by a simple realization. With happy tears in his eyes, the little boy who had been burned so badly that he had given up hope, expressed it like this: "They wouldn't send a special teacher to work on nouns and adverbs with a dying boy, now, would they?"

Excerpted from Moments for Mothers

Calvin and Hobbes   **by Bill Watterson**

How Could I Miss, I'm a Teacher!

You cannot teach people anything. You can only help them discover it within themselves.

Galileo

In the early 1960s in New York City, I worked with a group of eighth- and ninth-grade students who were only reading at the second- to third-grade level. I found it difficult not to experience despair, working with them, trying to tutor kids who had basically given up on school. Their attendance was spotty at best. I believe many of them came to school simply because this is where most of their friends were that day, rather than because they thought they might learn something.

Attitudinally, they were a disaster. Anger, cynicism, sarcasm and the expectation of being failed, ridiculed or put down was the tenor and content of their talk. I tried to tutor them in small groups and one-on-one, and I must confess the results were not encouraging with most. Oh, there were a few who seemed to respond more positively on an occasional basis, but it was impossible to tell when that marginally positive attitude might disappear, to be replaced by sullenness or unaccountable flashes of anger.

One of my other problems was the fact that, at the time, almost no age-appropriate remedial reading materials were available for junior high school students at such a low level. They wanted to read about relationships, dating, sports and cars, not materials like "Run, Spot, run! See the ball. It is bouncing." The kids regarded the materials I had as too babyish and beneath them. Unfortunately, more interesting materials were way too difficult in reading level for them to handle without much frustration. Several of them complained continuously about the reading material. Jose, a tall, lanky boy with a pronounced accent, captured the essence when he said, "Hey, man, this stuff is *boring*. And it's dumb, too! Why do we got to read this junk, man?"

A glimmer of an idea crept into my mind. I sought help from my department chairman on how to write a proposal for funding a little tutoring project. We didn't get a huge sum of money, but it was enough for a pilot program for the last six months of the school year. It was simple and it worked.

I "hired" my students as reading tutors. I told them that the nearby elementary school had students in the first, second and third grades who needed help in reading. I had some money that I could pay to anyone who'd help me work with these children. My students asked whether this would take place during or after school. "Oh, *during school*. In fact, it will be instead of our class period together. We'll just walk over there each day and work with the kids there.

"You've got to know, that if you don't show up, you don't get paid. And you also have to understand that it would be very disappointing to a young child if you were his or her tutor and you didn't show up or if you didn't work caringly with that child. You'll have a big responsibility!"

All but one of my 11 students jumped at the chance to be a part of this program. The lone holdout changed his mind within one week as he heard from the other students how much they were enjoying working with these young kids.

The elementary kids were grateful for the help but even more so for some attention from these older kids from their own neighborhood. Clearly you could see a version of hero worship in their eyes. Each of my students was assigned two or three younger children to work with. And they worked, reading to them and having them read aloud as well.

My goal was to find a way to legitimize eighth and ninth-graders reading such young material. I thought that, if I could get them to read that material and read regularly, they would surely improve. As it turned out, I was right. At the end of that year, testing showed almost all of them had improved one, two or even three grade levels in reading!

But the most spectacular changes were in my students' attitudes and behavior. I hadn't expected that they would start to dress better, with more care and more neatness. Nor had I expected that the number of fights would decrease while their attendance dramatically increased.

One morning, as I was entering school from the parking area, I saw Jose walking toward the door. He looked ill. "What's the matter, Jose?" I said, "You look like you might have a fever." This was a student whose attendance had been the second worst in the group.

"Oh, I guess I'm feeling kind of sick, Mr. McCarty," he replied.

"So why are you here today? Why didn't you stay home?" I asked.

His answer floored me. "Oh, man, I couldn't miss today, I'm a *teacher!* My students would miss me, wouldn't they?" He grinned and went in the building.

Hanoch McCarty

On That Note

It is the supreme art of the teacher to awaken joy in creative expression and knowledge.

Albert Einstein

One year when I was teaching second grade, a new child entered our class mid-year. His name was Daniel, and he brought a special light to our class.

Daniel came over to me one afternoon at the end of the school day. He said, "Ms. Johnson, I have a note for you from my old teacher. It's not on paper though, it's in my head." Daniel leaned over and said, "She wanted me to tell you how lucky you are to have me in your class!"

Krista Lyn Johnson

A Christmas Gift I'll
Never Forget

*A child's life is like a piece of paper on which
every passerby leaves a mark.*

Chinese Proverb

He entered my life 20 years ago, leaning against the doorjamb of Room 202, where I taught fifth grade. He wore sneakers three sizes too large and checkered pants ripped at the knees.

Daniel made this undistinguished entrance in the school of a quaint lakeside village known for its old money, white colonial homes and brass mailboxes. He told us his last school had been in a neighboring county. "We were pickin' fruit," he said matter-of-factly.

I suspected this friendly, scruffy, smiling boy from an emigrant family had no idea he had been thrown into a den of fifth-grade lions who had never before seen torn pants. If he noticed snickering, he didn't let on. There was no chip on his shoulder.

Twenty-five children eyed Daniel suspiciously until the kickball game that afternoon. Then he led off the first inning with a home run. With it came a bit of respect from the wardrobe critics of Room 202.

Next was Charles' turn. Charles was the least athletic, most overweight child in the history of fifth grade. After his second strike, amid the rolled eyes and groans of the class, Daniel edged up and spoke quietly to Charles' dejected back. "Forget them, kid. You can do it."

Charles warmed, smiled, stood taller and promptly struck out anyway. But at that precise moment, defying the social order of this jungle he had entered, Daniel gently began to change things—and us.

By autumn's end, we had all gravitated toward him. He taught us all kinds of lessons. How to call a wild turkey. How to tell whether fruit is ripe before that first bite. How to treat others, even Charles. Especially Charles. He never did use our names, calling me "Miss" and the students "kid."

The day before Christmas vacation, the students always brought gifts for the teacher. It was a ritual—opening each department-store box, surveying the expensive perfume or scarf or leather wallet, and thanking the child.

That afternoon, Daniel walked to my desk and bent close to my ear. "Our packing boxes came out last night," he said without emotion. "We're leavin' tomorrow."

As I grasped the news, my eyes filled with tears. He countered the awkward silence by telling me about the move. Then, as I regained my composure, he pulled a gray rock from his pocket. Deliberately and with great style, he pushed it gently across my desk.

I sensed that this was something remarkable, but all my practice with perfume and silk had left me pitifully unprepared to respond. "It's for you," he said, fixing his eyes on mine. "I polished it up special."

I've never forgotten that moment.

Years have passed since then. Each Christmas my daughter asks me to tell this story. It always begins after she picks up the small polished rock that sits on my desk. Then she nestles herself in my lap and I begin. The first words of the story never vary. "The last time I ever saw Daniel, he gave me this rock as a gift and told me about his boxes. That was a long time ago even before you were born.

"He's a grown-up now," I finish. Together we wonder where he is and what he has become.

"Someone good I bet," my daughter says. Then she adds, "Do the end of the story."

I know what she wants to hear—the lesson of love and caring learned by a teacher from a boy with nothing—and everything—to give. A boy who lived out of boxes. I touch the rock, remembering.

"Hi kid," I say softly. "This is Miss. I hope you no longer need the packing boxes. And Merry Christmas, wherever you are."

Linda DeMers Hummel

A Matter of Honor

One looks back with appreciation to the brilliant teachers, but with gratitude to those who touched our human feelings. The curriculum is so much necessary new material, but the warmth is the vital element for the growing plant and for the soul of the child.

Carl Jung

Since kindergarten, the staff at Abraham Lincoln and Thomas Edison elementary schools in Daly City, California, had seen the results of my mother's alcoholic outrage.

In the beginning, my teachers gently probed me about my paper-thin, shredded clothes, my offensive body odor, the countless bruises and burns on my arms, as well as why I hunted for food from garbage cans. One day my second-grade teacher, Ms. Moss, demanded a meeting with the school principal and pleaded with him to do something to help me. The principal reluctantly agreed to intervene. The next morning Mother and the principal had a private meeting. I never saw Ms. Moss again.

Immediately after that, things went from bad to worse. I was forced to live and sleep in the downstairs garage, ordered to perform slave-like chores, and received no food unless I met my mother's stringent time requirements for her demands. Mother had even changed my name from "David" to "It," and threatened to punish my brothers if they tried to sneak me food, use my real name or even look at me.

The only safe haven in my life were my teachers. They seemed to always go out of their way to make me feel like a *normal* child. Whenever one of them showered me with praise, I cherished every word. If one of my teachers brushed up against me as he or she bent over to check on my assignments, I absorbed the scent of their perfume or cologne. During the weekends, as I sat on top of my hands in the garage and shivered from the cold, I employed my secret weapon. I closed my eyes, took a deep breath and tried to picture my teacher's face. Only when I visualized my teacher's smile did I begin to feel warm inside.

But years later, one Friday afternoon, I lost control and stormed out of my fifth-grade homeroom class. I ran to the bathroom, pounded my tiny red fists against the tiles and broke down into a waterfall of tears. I was so frustrated because for months I could no longer see my saviors in my dreams. I desperately believed their life force had somehow kept me alive. But now, with no inner strength to draw upon, I felt so hollow and alone inside. Later that afternoon, once my peers scurried from the classroom to their homes or the playgrounds at hypersonic speeds, I dared myself and locked my eyes onto my homeroom teacher, Mr. Ziegler. For a fragment of time I knew he felt the immensity of my pain. A moment later I broke our stare, bowed my head in respect and turned away, somehow hoping for a miracle.

Months later my prayers were answered. On March 5, 1973, for some unknown reason, four teachers, the school nurse and the principal collectively decided to notify the authorities. Because of my condition, I was immediately placed into protective custody. But before I left, the entire staff, one by one, knelt down and held me. I knew by the look on everyone's faces that they were scared. My mind flashed back to the fate of Ms. Moss. I wanted to run away and dissolve. As a child called "It," I felt I was not worth their trouble.

As always my saviors sensed my anxiety and gave me a strong hug, as if to form an invisible shield to protect me from all harm. With each warm body I closed my eyes and tried to capture the moment for all eternity. With my eyes clamped shut, I heard one of my teachers gently whisper, "No matter the outcome, no matter what happens to us, this is something we had to do. As teachers . . . if we can have an effect on one child's life . . . This is the true meaning of our profession."

After a round of good-byes, I stood paralyzed—I had *never* in all my life felt such an outpouring of emotion for me. And with tears streaming down my cheeks, I promised the staff at Thomas Edison Elementary that I would never forget them and I would do my best to some-day make them proud.

Since my rescue, not a single day has passed that I have not thought about my saviors. Almost 20 years to the day, I returned to Thomas Edison Elementary and presented my teachers with the very first copies of my first book, *A Child Called "It,"* which was dedicated to them, and was published on the 20-year anniversary of my rescue—March 5, 1993. That evening my teachers sat in the front row of a capacity-filled auditorium, as I fulfilled my lifetime dream of making my teachers feel special. I looked at them, with tears now running down their faces, and said, "As a child I learned that teachers have but one goal: to some-how make a difference in the life of a child. In my case it was four teachers, my school nurse and my principal who fought and risked their careers to save the life of a child called 'It.' I cannot, nor will not, ever forget their courage and their conviction. Twenty years ago I made a promise to my teachers. And tonight I renew my vow. For me it is not a matter of maintaining a pledge to those who had an effect on my life. For me, it is simply a matter of honor."

Dave Pelzer

The Lesson Plan

The art of life lies in a constant readjustment to our surroundings.

Okakura Kukuzo

It was just an ordinary day. The children came to school on buses; there was the usual hubbub of excitement as they greeted each other. I looked over my plan book and I never felt better prepared to face the day. It would be a good day, I knew, and we would accomplish a lot. We took our places around the reading table and settled in for a good reading class. The first thing on my agenda was to check workbooks to see that the necessary work had been completed.

When I came to Troy, he had his head down as he shoved his unfinished assignment in front of me. He tried to pull himself back out of my sight as he sat on my right-hand side. Naturally, I looked at the incomplete work and said, "Troy, this is not finished."

He looked up at me with the most pleading eyes I have seen in a child and said, "I couldn't do it last night 'cuz my mother is dying."

The sobs that followed startled the entire class. How glad I was that he was sitting next to me. Yes, I took him in my arms and his head rested against my chest. There was no doubt in anyone's mind that Troy was hurting, hurting so much that I was afraid his little heart would break. His sobs echoed through the room and tears flowed copiously. The children sat with tear-filled eyes in dead silence. Only Troy's sobs broke the stillness of that morning class. One child raced for the Kleenex box while I just pressed his little body closer to my heart. I could feel my blouse being soaked by those precious tears. Helplessly, my tears fell upon his head.

The question that confronted me was, "What do I do for a child who is losing his mother?" The only thought that came to my mind was, "Love him . . . show him you care . . . cry with him." It seemed as though the whole bottom was coming out of his young life, and I could do little to help him. Choking back my tears, I said to the group, "Let us say a prayer for Troy and his mother." A more fervent prayer never floated to heaven. After some time, Troy looked up at me and said, "I think I will be okay now." He had exhausted his supply of tears; he released the burden in his heart. Later that afternoon, Troy's mother died.

When I went to the funeral parlor, Troy rushed to greet me. It was as though he had been waiting for me, that he expected I would come. He fell into my arms and just rested there awhile. He seemed to gain strength and courage, and then he led me to the coffin. There he was able to look into the face of his mother, to face death even though he might never be able to understand the mystery of it.

That night I went to bed thanking God that he had given me the good sense to set aside my reading plan and to hold the broken heart of a child in my own heart.

Sister Carleen Brennan

In Praise of Teachers

*What sculpture is to a block of marble, educa-
tion is to the soul.*

Joseph Addison

In 1972, I returned to Miami Beach High School to
speak to the drama class. Afterward I asked the drama
teacher if any of my English teachers are still there. Irene
Roberts, he tells me, is in class just down the hall.

I was no one special in Miss Roberts' class—just
another jock who did okay work. I don't recall any one
special bit of wisdom she passed on. Yet I cannot forget
her respect for language, for ideas and for her students. I
realize now, many years later, that she is the quintessen-
tial selfless teacher. I'd like to say something to her, I say,
but I don't want to pull her from a class. Nonsense, he
says, she'll be delighted to see you.

The drama teacher brings Miss Roberts into the hallway where stands this 32-year-old man she last saw at 18.
"I'm Mark Medoff," I tell her. "You were my 12th-grade
English teacher in 1958." She cocks her head at me, as if
this angle might conjure me in her memory. And then,

though armed with a message I want to deliver in some perfect torrent of words, I can't think up anything more memorable than this: "I want you to know," I say, "you were important to me."

And there in the hallway, this slight and lovely woman, now nearing retirement age, this teacher who doesn't remember me, begins to weep; and she encircles me in her arms.

Remembering this moment, I begin to sense that everything I will ever know, everything I will ever pass to my students, to my children, is an inseparable part of an ongoing legacy of our shared wonder and eternal hope that we can, must, make ourselves better.

Irene Roberts holds me briefly in her arms and through her tears whispers against my cheek, "Thank you." And then, with the briefest of looks into my forgotten face, she disappears back into her classroom, returns to what she has done thousands of days through all the years of my absence.

On reflection, maybe those were, after all, just the right words to say to Irene Roberts. Maybe they are the very words I would like to speak to all those teachers I carry through my life as part of me, the very words I would like spoken to me one day by some returning student: "I want you to know you were important to me."

Mark Medoff

The Greatest Teacher of My Life

Parents learn a lot from their children about coping with life.

Muriel Spark

I had already been a teacher for 15 years when I met my greatest teacher. It wasn't in a classroom but in a hospital. She was my daughter Kelsey.

Kelsey was born with cerebral palsy, and at age five she faced a battle with cancer that she later won. She has taught me many vivid lessons about courage and determination, and I'm a better person forever because of her patience with me.

When she was four, she wanted to learn to tie her shoes just as her best friend had done. I was stumped. Because of her cerebral palsy, Kelsey has very little use of the fingers on her left hand. If I couldn't tie a shoe single-handedly, how was I going to teach her?

After three and a half years of persistence, Kelsey finally did it. I remember that first day of summer vacation, when she was seven and a half years old, as I watched and encouraged her. When she took her hand away to reveal two neatly worked loops, she beamed from ear to ear and I cried for joy. And the truth is, no one ever asks Kelsey how old she was when she learned to tie her shoes. I learned about determination from her accomplishment—and much more. Pace wasn't going to be the important thing in Kelsey's life—accomplishing her goals within her own timetable would be what mattered most.

Throughout her cancer treatment, Kelsey took charge of her circumstances through creative play. In the hospital, the game was always "restaurant," with Kelsey playing waitress and the rest of us cast as customers. For hours on end, she lost herself in the drama, as if we weren't in the hospital at all, but out in the world away from doctors and tests—a world Kelsey was certain she would be a part of someday.

At home, where she felt safer exploring deeper feelings, the play turned to "hospital." In this game Kelsey was doctor-in-charge for a change. Her game included medical terms even we adults didn't understand. We'd just play along, knowing that Kelsey had found a way to cope.

When she was six, she wanted to take ballet lessons. I'm embarrassed to admit how much this frightened me. Her muscles were weak from chemotherapy, she had poor balance, and her weight had slipped to 34 pounds. I wasn't just afraid for her body, but for her feelings. She had no fear at this point and wore a patch over one eye, so I worried about the teasing she might get from the rest of the dance class. But I didn't know how to tell Kelsey all of this, and she wouldn't let up, so I enrolled her in a ballet school.

Kelsey danced with abandon! Did she fall? Of course. Was she awkward? Very. But she was never self-conscious or inhibited, throwing herself into the process, completely unaffected by what she couldn't do. The sheer joy of dancing was enough. Every person who saw Kelsey dance came away with something special. She danced for four years. When she quit, it was only to announce that she wanted to take horseback riding lessons instead. This time I enrolled her without hesitating.

In fifth grade, Kelsey excitedly brought home a registration form for intramural basketball. Now this was going to be a major challenge for her. She could run only slowly, she's short, and she still had the use of only one hand. Bells of caution went off inside my head again, but I had learned to ignore them. The excitement in her eyes emphatically canceled out all the drawbacks, and we signed her up.

After the first practice the coach said that he was afraid to let her play in a game. When he explained how she might get hurt, I could see visions of lawsuits dancing in his head. But every child who plays sports takes risks, I reasoned with him, and if her risk was greater, her need to belong was greater still. After a few discussions and a little more encouragement, he decided to let her play. For two years, Kelsey played harder than any girl in the league. And while she never made a basket during a game, she brought other gifts that were more valuable to her teammates. In two years, I never once saw a player treat her as anything other than an asset. And after weeks of trying, when Kelsey finally made her first basket during practice, every girl in the entire gym—from *both* teams—stopped and applauded.

On game days, when we stopped at the grocery store, Kelsey quickly shed her winter coat and flung it into the grocery cart. It took me a while to realize why. She was so proud of her team shirt, she didn't want it to go un - noticed. Now Kelsey wasn't just winning her own personal triumphs, she was part of a team, too.

Today, Kelsey is a happy, healthy seventh grader, still lapping up life, trying new challenges, and still teaching her friends and parents a lot about persistence, the power of belief and compassion.

Kelsey, I'll never have a greater teacher!

Dauna Easley

The Thought Card

Everything can be taken from a man but one thing: the last of the human freedoms—to choose one's own way.

Viktor Frankl

I must admit that I was still an angry adolescent in my first years of college. My anger was diffuse—the world didn't please me in almost any way. My anger was focused—my parents didn't please me at all. I chafed under my father's direction and correction.

With limited finances, I chose to go to a local college and commute to classes every day. One day I had a serious fight with my father. I felt he was trying to control me, and I wanted to break free. He saw me as rebellious and tried to reassert his authority. We both exploded in shouts. I stormed out of the house and missed my bus to school. I knew that catching the next bus meant I would be late to my education class. That made me even more furious.

I fumed and sighed all the way to school. My mind was racing with angry thoughts about my father. Like many adolescents, I was stuck in my egocentricity—certain that no one in the world had ever had such a terrible father nor had anyone had to contend with such unfairness. After all, my father hadn't even finished high school and here I was, a mighty *college student!* I felt so superior to him. How dare he interfere with my life and my plans?

As I ran across the sprawling campus toward the building where my class met, I suddenly realized that I didn't have the assignment that was due: *a thought card.*

This class was taught by Dr. Sidney B. Simon, one of the most unusual teachers at the school. His policies and procedures were unique, his grading policy revolutionary, his teaching methods unsettling. People *talked* about Dr. Simon.

During our first class, Professor Simon explained, "Every Tuesday, you must bring in a 4" x 6" index card with your name and the date on the top line. As for what's on the rest of the card, that's up to you. You can write a thought, a concern, a feeling, a question or just plain anything that's on your mind. It's your way of communicating with me directly. These cards will be completely confidential. I will return them to you every Wednesday. You'll find that I will write comments on your cards. If you ask a question, I'll do my level best to answer it. If you have a concern, I will respond to that as best I can. But remember, this card is your ticket of admission to class on Tuesdays."

On the first Tuesday of the class, I dutifully brought in my index card with my name and the date written carefully on the top line. I then added, "All that glitters is not gold." The following day, Dr. Simon returned the cards to the class. Mine had a penciled note, "What does this quote mean to you? Is it significant?" This comment made me uneasy. Apparently he was taking these cards seriously. I surely didn't want to reveal myself to him.

The week progressed. The course met every day for one hour. Dr. Simon was quite brilliant. He taught by asking questions, raising issues that none of my teachers had ever raised before. He challenged us to think and to think deeply. Social issues, political issues, personal issues all were grist for the mill in this class. It was a class in methods of teaching social studies and it was far-ranging. The teachers I had in high school taught social studies—history, geography, economics and so on, as rote subjects, lists of facts and names and dates to be memorized and returned to paper on exams. Rarely had anyone asked us to think.

At first, I thought he was going to propagandize us for or against something, but not Professor Simon. Instead, he simply asked us to think, explore, research, question and then come up with our own responses. Frankly, I became even more uncomfortable. There was something delightful, refreshing and inviting about his teaching, but since I had rarely experienced this style, I had no "coping strategies" to help me deal with him. I knew how to do well in a class: sit up front, tell the teacher how much you "enjoyed" the lecture, turn in neat typed papers written according to a formula and memorize, memorize, memorize! This class was clearly something different. I couldn't use these time-worn, time-tested methods to pass.

The second Tuesday came. I wrote on my card, "A stitch in time gathers no moss." Again, not trusting him, I covered myself with humor, which had always been my best defense against unwanted closeness. The next day the card came back with this note: "You seem to have a sense of humor. Is this an important part of your life?"

What did he want? What was going on here? I couldn't remember a teacher caring personally about me since elementary school. What did this man want?

Now, I raced down the hallway, 10 minutes late to class. Just outside the door, I took an index card from my notebook and wrote my name and the date on it. Desperate for something to write on it, I could only think about the fight I'd just had with my dad. "I am the son of an idiot!" I wrote and then dashed into the room. He stood, conducting a discussion, near the door. Looking up at me, he reached out for the card and I handed it to him and took my seat.

The moment I reached my seat, I felt overwhelmed with dread. What had I done? I gave him that card! Oh, no! I didn't mean to let that out. Now he'll know about my anger, about my dad, about my life! I don't remember anything about the rest of that class session. All I could think about was the card.

I had difficulty sleeping that night, filled with a nameless dread. What could these cards be all about? Why did I tell him that about my dad? Suppose he contacts my dad? What business is it of his anyway?

Wednesday morning arrived and I reluctantly got ready for school. When I got to the class, I was early. I wanted to sit in back and hide as best I could. The class began and Dr. Simon began giving back the thought cards. He put mine on the desk face down as was his usual practice. I picked it up, almost unable to turn it over.

When I looked at the face of the card, he had written, "What does the 'son of an idiot' do with the rest of his life?" It felt like someone had punched me in the stomach. I had spent a lot of time hanging out in the student union cafeteria talking with other young men about the problems I had "because of my parents." And they, too, shared the same sort of material with me. No one challenged anyone to take responsibility for himself. No, we all accepted the parent-blaming game with relief. Everything was our parents' fault. If we did poorly on tests, blame Mom. If we just missed getting a student-aid job, blame Dad. I constantly complained about my folks and all the guys nodded sagely. These folks who were paying the tuition were certainly an interfering bunch of fools, weren't they?

Sidney Simon's innocent-seeming question punctured that balloon. It got right to the heart of the issue: Whose problem is it? Whose responsibility are you?

I skipped going to the student union that day and went straight home, strangely depressed, chastened. All evening I thought about it and about something my mother had said: "The millionaire calls himself a 'self-made man,' but if he gets arrested, he blames his abusive parents."

I wish I could say that I experienced a magical transformation but it wasn't true. However, Dr. Simon's comment was insidious. It kept coming up in my mind over the next few weeks. Again and again, as I heard myself blaming my father for this or that, a little internal voice said, "Okay, suppose your father is all those bad things you said. How long do you think you can get away with blaming him for your life?"

Slowly, inexorably, my thinking shifted. I heard myself blaming a lot. After a while, I realized that I had created a life in which I was not a central figure! I was the object of the action, not the subject. That felt even more uncomfortable than any feeling I had in Dr. Simon's class. I didn't want to be a puppet. I wanted to be an actor, not a re-actor. The process of growth wasn't easy or fast. It took over a year before people noticed that I was taking responsibility for my own actions, my own choices, my own feelings. I was surprised at how my grades improved in all my subjects. I was astounded at the increase in the number—and quality—of my friends. I was equally astonished by how much smarter my father seemed.

All through this process, I kept sending in my thought cards. Later, I took another course with this unique teacher. I worked harder for him than I had in any other class I had ever taken. With each thought card came more unsettling questions for thought.

Several years later, I was astounded at my own progress. From a struggling, marginal student I became a successful student and then a successful high school teacher. I went from constant anger and constant avoidance of the necessary work in my life to someone who was energized, excited, purposeful and even joyful.

My relationship with my father also improved dramatically. Instead of controlling, now I saw him as concerned and caring. I recognized that he didn't have "smooth" ways of parenting me but that his intentions were very loving. The fights diminished and finally disappeared. I learned to see my father as a smart, wise and loving man. And it all started with a question, an innocent-seeming question.

Hanoch McCarty

5

ON DEATH AND DYING

Life is eternal; and love is immortal; and death is only a horizon; and a horizon is nothing save the limit of our sight.

Rossiter Worthington Raymond

A Treasure in Time

*They that love beyond the world cannot be sep-
arated by it. Death cannot kill what never dies.*

William Penn

Interstate 40 stretched endlessly before me. I was coming home from the first family reunion without Bob, held
in June of 1995. Memories of our short nine years of marriage flooded through me.

We both worked for the Social Security Administration
and three years previously accepted positions in a field
office in Oklahoma City, a transfer we needed for any
future advancements. In February 1995, a 10-week training session for a promotion sent me to Dallas, Texas; a session cut short by the news of a bomb ripping through the
Alfred P. Murrah Building in Oklahoma City.

My Bob was in that building.

When Bob and I first met, he was putting together a
tape of love songs titled "20 Years of Loving You," gleaned
from albums and 45s borrowed from friends, some of
whom were unattached women with their own agenda.

I offered him the use of my record collection and asked him to use my favorite, Stevie Wonder's "I Just Called to Say I Love You."

By the time Bob finished the tape, we had been dating for several weeks. One Saturday, he called and said he had a surprise for me. As I got in the car and we headed for the highway, he took out a cassette and slid his finished tape into the tape deck. My own voice, taken from a message I once left on his answering machine, came out of the speaker: "I just called . . ." The tape then faded into the music of Stevie Wonder. "This one is especially for you," he said.

The memory brought tears to my eyes. Now, close to the Oklahoma state line, I happened to see the sign "Oklahoma Trading Post—50 Miles Ahead—Exit 287." It occurred to me that Bob and I always meant to stop on our return trips from his family reunions in Florida, but we never did. We had already gassed up an exit or two before, we were tired, we just wanted to get home. "This time," I decided, "I'm going to stop."

As I drove, my mind wandered; how could I ever make it without Bob—my big, strong husband whose comforting arms held me when I cried, whose sense of humor melted my anger, and whose sense of adventure enriched both our lives. Tears stained my cheeks, but I kept driving. Suddenly, there was exit 287. Damn! I had passed the Trading Post. Well, maybe next time.

Just as suddenly as I made the decision to drive on, I decided I would go back! I swerved the car at the last instant and drove up the ramp. Reaching the main road, I realized I was on the Turner Turnpike—no exits for who knew how many miles. I looked for a flat place in the median and drove across, mindless of whether a state trooper might be watching, and headed back toward the Trading Post.

As expected, the Trading Post was like many Bob and I stopped at on our travels: a mixture of Southwestern goods and souvenirs. As I wandered through the store, I came upon a wrought-iron and wooden bed setup showcasing Indian blankets, prickly cactus plants and strings of red and green peppers.

Beside the bed was a small table holding Aztec vases, delicate desert flowers and a howling coyote with a bright scarf around its neck. Unobtrusively nestled among them sat a small, old-timey wooden telephone with a carved mouthpiece and rotary dial, its receiver resting on the black prong and connected with a thin black cord. My first thought was, "How unusual. Everything else is so Southwestern, the telephone looks out of place." Picking it up, I lifted the receiver.

A musical tinkling began from the base of the phone. Tears filled my eyes and coursed down my cheeks. A wave of warmth swept over me as I stood sobbing, clutching the phone, oblivious of other customers walking warily around me. The tune I heard was "I Just Called to Say I Love You."

Making my way toward the front to pay for my newfound treasure, there was no doubt now that I could make it. I was not alone; my Bob had just called to say he loved me.

Judy Walker

You Don't Bring Me Flowers, Anymore

*P*ain *and suffering is inevitable, being miserable is optional.*

Art Clanin

The elderly caretaker of a peaceful lonely cemetery received a check every month from a woman, an invalid in a hospital in a nearby city. The check was to buy fresh flowers for the grave of her son, who had been killed in an automobile accident a couple of years before.

One day a car drove into the cemetery and stopped in front of the caretaker's ivy-covered administration building. A man was driving the car. In the back seat sat an elderly lady, pale as death, her eyes half-closed.

"The lady is too ill to walk," the driver told the caretaker. "Would you mind coming with us to her son's grave—she has a favor to ask of you. You see, she is dying, and she has asked me, as an old family friend, to bring her out here for one last look at her son's grave."

"Is this Mrs. Wilson?" the caretaker asked.

The man nodded.

"Yes, I know who she is. She's the one who has been sending me a check every month to put flowers on her son's grave." The caretaker followed the man to the car and got in beside the woman. She was frail and obviously near death. But there was something else about her face, the caretaker noted—the eyes dark and sullen, hiding some deep, long-lasting hurt.

"I am Mrs. Wilson," she whispered. "Every month for the past two years—"

"Yes, I know. I have attended to it, just as you asked."

"I have come here today," she went on, "because the doctors tell me I have only a few weeks left. I shall not be sorry to go. There is nothing left to live for. But before I die, I wanted to come here for one last look and to make arrangements with you to keep on placing the flowers on my son's grave."

She seemed exhausted—the effort to speak sapping her strength. The car made its way down a narrow, gravel road to the grave. When they reached the grave, the woman, with what appeared to be great effort, raised herself slightly and gazed out the window at her son's tombstone. There was no sound during the moments that followed—only the chirping of the birds in the tall, old trees scattered among the graves.

Finally, the caretaker spoke. "You know, Ma'am, I was always sorry you kept sending the money for the flowers."

The woman seemed at first not to hear. Then slowly she turned toward him. "Sorry?" she whispered. "Do you realize what you are saying—my son . . ."

"Yes, I know," he said gently. "But, you see, I belong to a church group that every week visits hospitals, asylums, prisons. There are live people in those places who need cheering up, and most of them love flowers—they can see

them and smell them. That grave—" he said, "over there—
there's no one living, no one to see and smell the beauty
of the flowers . . ." he looked away, his voice trailing off.

The woman did not answer, but just kept staring at the
grave of her son. After what seemed like hours, she lifted
her hand and the man drove them back to the caretaker's
building. He got out and without a word they drove off.
I've offended her, he thought. *I shouldn't have said what I did.*

Some months later, however, he was astonished to
have another visit from the woman. This time there was
no driver. She was driving the car herself! The caretaker
could hardly believe his eyes.

"You were right," she told him, "about the flowers.
That's why there have been no more checks. After I got
back to the hospital, I couldn't get your words out of my
mind. So I started buying flowers for the others in the
hospital who didn't have any. It gave me such a feeling of
joy to see how much they enjoyed them—and from a total
stranger. It made them happy, but more than that, it made
me happy.

"The doctors don't know," she went on, "what is suddenly making me well, but I do!"

Bits & Pieces

The Grave
No One Tended

The day was lovely as I strolled along
  peering at stones on the way,
And that's when I saw it, that pitiful cross
  that looked splintered and faded away.

With flowers in hand to tend Father's grave,
  I knew I must hurry along.
But I couldn't help but linger awhile
  at that cross that just didn't belong.

The date on the front confirmed my suspicions
  of what already I knew.
A child lay beneath that horrible cross
  and its faded color of blue.

What selfish parents they must have been
  to bury their child all alone,
Without flowers or candles to light the night
  and not even a simple headstone.

I looked even closer at that awful cross
   that was nearly splintered away,
And there on the back, I read the words
   that changed me forever that day.

"This cross isn't grand, but it was carved by my hands
   so you'll know, son, how much I care.
It's the color of blue to remind me of you
   and how painful it is I'm not there,

That it's you who is gone and it's me living on
   while your young life has come to an end.
And I'm left alone, never again with a home
   and a grave that's too painful to tend."

Tears stung my eyes as I looked all around
   at the monuments that ragged cross put to shame.
And I shared with those parents their horrible loss
   that brought them such terrible pain.

And all the tombstones, some even taller than me
   suddenly seemed small in a way,
Next to that little handmade cross, carved with such love
   and the flowers I planted that day.

Cheryl L. Costello-Forshey

The Donor

Signs from the soul come silently, as silently as the sun enters the darkened world.

Tibetan Saying

My grown daughter, Sara, and I were very good friends. She lived with her family in a nearby town which allowed us to see each other very often. In between visits we wrote or talked on the phone.

When she called me, she always said, "Hi, Mom, it's me," and I'd say, "Hi, Me, how are you today?" She often signed her letters simply, "Me." Sometimes I'd call her "Me" just to tease.

Then my poor Sara died suddenly, without warning, from a brain hemorrhage. Needless to say, I was devastated! There can be no worse pain for a parent than to lose a beloved child. It took all my considerable faith to keep going.

We decided to donate her organs so at least that much good could come from such an otherwise tragic situation. In due time, I heard from the Organ Retrieval Group telling me where all her organs went. No names were mentioned, of course.

About one year later, I received a beautiful letter from the young man who received her pancreas and kidney. What a difference it made in his life!

Praise God! And since he couldn't use his own name, guess how he signed his letter: "Me"!

My cup runneth over.

Mary M. Jelinek

Red Jell-O at Dawn

Family means sharing inadequacies, imperfections and feelings with each other and still loving each other. But even when you set out to love, you may not always be a likable person. And when you're not perfect, forgiveness for yourself and others becomes important. Then you get up the next day and start again. It is a process, like the opening of a bud. It is a flowering, a blooming and blossoming.

Bernie Siegel

When my youngest child, Andrew, was 11 years old, he asked if we could have a "ceremony" at the lake to commemorate the second anniversary of his dad's death. I didn't know what to think. He not only wanted us to watch the sunrise in silence at the shore of Lake Michigan, he also insisted that we eat red cherry Jell-O with bananas in it while we sat in the sand.

"Jell-O? At six in the morning?" I asked incredulously.

"Mom, red Jell-O with bananas was Dad's favorite snack. We always made it together when I visited him on weekends."

I still had hurt feelings that Harold filed for divorce two months into our agreed-upon year-long separation without any effort at marriage counseling. And I was especially hurt that he remarried the day our divorce was final. When he died two years later, I helped Andrew through the grieving process while trying to ignore my own feelings. Now we had to bring it all up again?

"Andrew, it's supposed to be really cold tomorrow. Couldn't you just think about your dad at home?"

"Mom, please, it'll be okay. I just want us to sit there on the sand and eat the Jell-O and think about Dad. We can dress warm and we'll take a blanket."

I thought I'd done a good job of helping Andrew adjust to his father's death these past two years as I tried to be the best "only" parent a child could have. But I wasn't sure about this early morning ceremony thing at the beach. As he waited for my answer, the pleading look on his face told me how much his idea meant to him.

"All right, Andrew," I said reluctantly. "We'll have to get up at 5:15 if you want to get there while it's still dark."

"No problem, Mom! I'll set my alarm. Do you think Wayne would come if I ask him?"

I wondered what Wayne, the man I'd been dating for a couple of months, would think about Andrew's plan. Wayne's wife had died just two months after Harold, and I knew Wayne was still dealing with his own grief. I didn't know if it was fair to drag him along to Andrew's strange beach ceremony.

That afternoon, Wayne stopped by the house while I was stirring the red Jell-O. Andrew launched into his plan.

"So, Wayne, do you want to go? The sunrise will be great!"

"Sure, Andrew, I'm glad you asked me."

I shot Wayne a look that said, "Are you sure about this?" Then I said, "Do you realize it's going to be only 20 degrees tomorrow morning? With the wind off the lake, the wind-chill factor will probably be below zero!"

Wayne smiled, "It'll be a great adventure."

The next morning as Wayne pulled up in front of our house, Andrew and I greeted him in our full winter gear. Both of us were wearing jogging suits under our heavy winter coats, hats and mittens. I had earmuffs on under my hat.

I tossed an old green bedspread into Wayne's van then retrieved the Jell-O from the refrigerator.

A few minutes later, in the pitch dark, we arrived at Grant Park Beach in South Milwaukee, the only humans in sight. *Naturally,* I thought, *nobody else in his right mind would be here at this time in this cold!*

Wayne and Andrew smoothed the bedspread on the sand about 30 feet from the jet black water. We snuggled close to the front of the bedspread and pulled the back half up around our bodies as a windbreak.

For a few minutes, Andrew's "silence" rule made me uncomfortable. But then I looked at Wayne and Andrew and knew that they were both remembering and missing the person they had loved so much in life.

I knew Wayne was thinking about the wonderful relationship he'd had with his beloved Janet, his wife of 31 years. And without a doubt, Andrew was thinking about Harold. About the walks they took along the lake. About the plays and concerts his father had taken him to. About their trip to Florida just two months before he died.

I looked at them, concentrating on those warm, wonderful memories and suddenly my heart softened. *Could it be that Andrew is on to something by having this ceremony?* I wondered.

I pulled the green spread tighter around my neck and recalled a verse in Philippians 4:8 that said: "Fix your thoughts on what is true and good and right. Think about things that are pure and lovely, and dwell on the fine, good things in others. Think about all you can praise God for and be glad about."

I recalled the happy, early days of my marriage to Harold. The bike rides, teaching Harold to ice skate, the two wonderful trips to Arizona to visit his sister and brother and their families.

I remembered when Andrew was born, in Harold's 51st year, and how proud he was of his new son. Why, he'd passed out cigars the day he found out I was pregnant!

I recalled how scared I was when Harold had emergency gallbladder surgery a few years after we were married. I remembered how I laughed when he dressed up in a crazy red plaid sportcoat and too-short, orange plaid pants for "nerd day" at the high school where he was principal.

Suddenly, the unhappy times in our marriage faded away and as I watched a line of pink and steel blue clouds inching their way onto the horizon, I felt as if a dam had broken. All the good memories that I'd buried the day Harold moved out of our home came rushing back.

I pulled the bedspread tighter around my neck and snuggled closer to Andrew, who had his head on my chest, trying to keep the cold away. The more I thought about Harold, the more I realized how much I missed him.

Even though it was still 20 minutes or so until the actual sunrise, the intensity of sunlight from below the horizon was filling the beach with an eerie sense of "almost" day. And I was filled with an eerie sense of "almost" peace.

Andrew motioned that it was time to eat the Jell-O. I took the lid off the container. When I placed a spoon into Wayne's hand, I squeezed his fingers through bulky gloves. He smiled and I knew he understood what was going on in my mind and in Andrew's.

And so we three ate red Jell-O at dawn on the shore of Lake Michigan in a wind chill that felt very close to zero degrees. But somehow I wasn't shivering. And the Jell-O tasted good.

Just as the sun popped up on the horizon in a magnificent display of color, Wayne and Andrew stood up.

"It's okay to talk now," Andrew said.

Wayne put his big arms around Andrew and held him close. "I know what you're going through, Son. I loved my wife very much, just like you loved your dad. And it's a wonderful thing to take time to cherish those memories."

I stood up as the full ball of wild orange sun now rested precariously and breathtakingly beautiful on the horizon line. "Andrew, let's walk along the shore for a few minutes."

"Good idea," Wayne smiled. "I'll go warm up the van."

As Andrew and I walked hand in hand along the edge of the water, we talked about his dad. Andrew picked up pebbles and tossed them as far as he could throw.

"I love you, Dad!" he shouted to the wind.

It was time to leave. When we arrived back at our house, Andrew announced that he was going to fix his specialty, "French toast for everyone!"

Later, as we clinked our glasses of orange juice and toasted Harold Lorenz, I knew that because of this sensitive 11-year-old child, I'd not only been led into a strange world of ceremony and silence—I'd been given the chance to grieve openly for the first time and to "dwell on the fine, good things in others." After that day, it seemed easier to praise God for everything in my life that is "true and good and right"—including a very special young son named Andrew.

Patricia Lorenz

When We Give Thanks

Kind words do not cost much. . . . Yet they accomplish much.

Blaise Pascal

We always celebrated Dad's November birthday on Thanksgiving Day, even after he entered a nursing home. As years went on, these events took on a double meaning for me—a traditional birthday party for Dad, and a personal thanking for all he had been to me in my life.

When we knew that it might be his last birthday, the whole family decided to rearrange Thanksgiving plans and come together for a huge Grandpa Simon birthday celebration at the nursing home. It was a crowded party with lots of noise and abundant food. Dad was having the time of his life. He was a marvelous storyteller, and here was the biggest captive audience he'd ever had. The party crackled around him.

During a quiet moment, I announced that it was now Dad's turn to listen to some stories for a change. I wanted everyone to tell Grandpa Simon what we loved about him. The room became still, and even Dad was quiet as his family crowded around him, like subjects around the throne.

One after another, people told stories from their hearts, while Dad listened with wet, flashing blue eyes. People recalled all kinds of lost memories—stories about when they were little, stories about when Dad was young, stories that are shared family treasures. Then someone told the story of Mother and the vase . . .

My mother was a short stocky woman, who always bent over the table to read the newspaper. Leaning her elbows on the table to support her chin, her body made a perfect right angle. One night, Dad placed her precious gold-plated vase, a family heirloom, right on her fanny at her body's angle. She couldn't move, couldn't stop from laughing, and screamed for help through her tears, while the vase teetered precariously. We all rolled on the floor laughing until Dad finally rescued the vase.

The stories flowed. Each one seemed to trigger the memory of two more. Even the littlest grandchildren couldn't wait to tell Dad why they loved him. For a man who had been kind to so many hundreds of people in his life, here was our chance to celebrate him.

A few months later, at Dad's memorial service, we more fully realized what we had given Dad that night. Those were the stories people normally tell at a funeral, after a loved one is no longer around to hear the words. They are told, then, full of tears, with the hope that the departed will somehow hear the outpouring of love. But we had given those loving memories to Dad in life, told through laughter, accompanied by hugs and joy. He had them to hold and roll over in his mind during his last months and days.

Words do matter, and they are enough. We just need to say them, to speak them publicly to the ones we love, for everyone else to hear. That's the way to give back love, and our chance to celebrate a person in life.

Sidney B. Simon

A Mother Is Waiting

God could not be everywhere, and so he made mothers!

Jewish Proverb

John Todd was born in Rutledge, Vermont, into a family of several children. They later moved to the village of Killingsworth back in the early 1880s. There, at a very early age, both of John's parents died.

One dear and loving aunt said she would take little John. The aunt sent a horse and a servant, Caesar, to get John who was only six at this time. On the way back, this endearing conversation took place.

John: Will she be there?

Caesar: Oh, yes, she'll be there waiting up for you.

John: Will I like living with her?

Caesar: My son, you fall into good hands.

John: Will she love me?

Caesar: Ah, she has a big heart.

John: Will I have my own room? Will she let me have a puppy?

Caesar: She's got everything all set, Son. I think she has some surprises, John.

John: Do you think she'll go to bed before we get there?

Caesar: Oh, no! She'll be sure to wait up for you. You'll see when we get out of these woods. You'll see her candle in the window.

Sure enough, as they neared the house, John saw a candle in the window and his aunt standing in the doorway. As he shyly approached the porch, she reached down, kissed him, and said, "Welcome home!"

John Todd grew up in his aunt's home and later became a great minister. She was mother to him. She gave him a second home.

Years later his aunt wrote to tell John of her own impending death because of failing health. She wondered what would become of her.

This is what John Todd wrote in reply:

> My Dear Aunt,
> Years ago, I left a house of death, not knowing where I was to go, whether anyone cared, whether it was the end of me. The ride was long, but the servant encouraged me. Finally I arrived to your embrace and a new home. I was expected; I felt safe. You did it all for me.
> Now it's your turn to go. I'm writing to let you know, someone is waiting up, your room is all ready, the light is on, the door is open, and you're expected! I know. I once saw God standing in your doorway . . . long ago!

Excerpted from Moments for Mothers

I Thought You'd Want to Know

We must not only give what we have; we must also give what we are.

Desiré-Joseph Mercier

Diane Weinman suffered an unbearable loss—the death of her 17-year-old daughter, Katie, in an auto accident. In the midst of her grief, she received a letter from the sheriff's deputy who had been at the scene. The letter made the loss a little more bearable for her and her husband.

> *Mr. & Mrs. Weinman,*
>
> *I am sorry for your loss. I am writing this letter to you because I have three teenage children of my own, a son and two daughters. If any of them died, I would want to know the things that I am going to tell you.*
>
> *I came upon the accident scene on an icy stretch of road. Katie was in the driver's seat. She had received a severe blow to the left side of her head, and the force had rendered her unconscious. I lifted her head to ease her breathing; then I held her gently and kindly until the rescue personnel arrived. After a few minutes, it was*

clear that Katie did not survive, but we did not stop helping her breathe until an electronic monitor was connected to her and verified that she was gone.

I wanted you to know that Katie was not awake and frightened and suffering—she never regained consciousness. I also wanted you to know that she did not die alone. She died being held by a father who loves his own teenage daughters, and knows how precious children are. I am sorry this happened to your little girl. Please call me if you should ever wish to talk about that day.

Prayerfully,
Robert Gross
Lane County Sheriff's Department

Not surprisingly, the Weinmans did want to meet Gross. This happened at Katie's funeral. "Then a few weeks later he stopped by to visit, stayed for two hours and answered every question I had," Diane Weinman said later. "It helped so much, because he's a dad and he knew my pain. He was direct and honest—and he has a strong faith. He made a big difference. Even in my pain, he told me what I wanted to know."

Karen Nordling McCowan

Matt's Story

All, everything that I understand, I understand only because I love.

Leo Tolstoy

I was grieving. I was grieving because recently my doctor told me I had multiple sclerosis, an unpredictable disease that can wreak havoc with the central nervous system. But I couldn't only grieve for myself. My good friend, Matt Bennett, had just died.

The phone rang at seven o'clock Saturday morning. Matt's father, Jesse, spoke quietly, "We lost Matt in the middle of the night."

Matt had been, and always will be, my role model. He was a lion of courage. I met him when he was 13 when I was asked to cover his story by my newspaper, a Los Angeles daily. Matt had been diagnosed with neuro - blastoma, a fatal cancer that would eventually course its way from his stomach through his entire body.

It wasn't a story a newspaper normally covered, but what intrigued us was that Matt wouldn't quit his baseball league. He just kept playing ball, struggling along despite his pain, still filled with a sense of humor. He was a large boy. His own mother called him an ox, and when I first met him he gleefully whipped off his baseball cap to proudly show me his bald head after chemotherapy.

He was one of a kind, our Matt. Here I was a reporter, but I couldn't help getting close to this family. I lost all sense of objectivity. Forget it. There was so much love between Matt and his mother, Billie, you could feel its intensity when you walked into their house—or wherever they were together. She left her job and cared for Matt every day of his life, including the times he decided to try the next experimental drug and she heard him screaming in pain from the next room.

"There's still hope, Mom," he always told her.

His story is one of courage because he never gave up. I knew Matt for three years, from age 13 to 16. I was there when he graduated from junior high school, and I wrote a story about it. I visited him at home and at the hospital. When it was apparent that I myself was ill, Matt was there for me. He wanted to come to the hospital and hold my hand while I went through tests. He explained it pretty much like: "I've been there. I understand. I've done all that."

One evening toward the end of his life, I went with my husband to visit Matt at the hospital. He was watching his favorite team, the Oakland A's, and his favorite player, Mark McGwire. (McGwire did take the time to meet Matt, for which his family is eternally grateful.) That was odd, because Matt couldn't really see the television. He was going blind from the cancer, but you would never know it. He commented on every play and told us how proud he was of McGwire.

The next moment was one of the most powerful in my life. Matt turned, looked at me as though he could see me and announced in the crowded room: "Diana, I love you."

I was amazed that a 16-year-old boy could say that, and at that moment I realized he had changed from a boy into a man. I loved Matt. Forget journalism. Forget the rule that reporters are supposed to be objective. When you meet someone like Matt, there's no such thing. There's only love. I hugged him good-bye and said I'd be back.

Before I could, the phone call came. My husband clutched me in his arms and held me while I cried.

Later that day we went to the florist to send the family a plant. I was shaking when we walked in and felt like collapsing.

I gave the florist the address, and she asked me for the phone number.

"I don't have it with me," I said.

"Well, I can't send it without the number," she explained politely. "We have to make sure they're home to receive it."

Now I panicked. "Call information," I responded, but I knew in my heart that the Bennetts weren't listed. The florist called as we stood there, tension filling the air. I began to feel really sick.

As my husband and I watched her on the phone, we saw a strange look come over her face. The look was so peculiar and she was actually engaging in a conversation with the operator. When the florist got off the phone, she looked at us in stunned surprise and said: "They aren't listed. But the operator is their next-door neighbor. She promised to make sure they received the plant."

The moment was quiet. We all looked at each other.

Immediately, I calmed down because I knew somehow Matt was still with me, trying to keep me calm. Three years later, he is still with me—at least in my heart. I keep his photo with me in my bedroom. When I'm sick and miserable, I think: "How would Matt handle this?"

Diana L. Chapman

To All Parents

I'll lend you for a little time a child of mine, He said,
For you to love the while she lives and mourn for when
    she's dead.
It may be six or seven years, or twenty-two or three,
But will you, till I call her back, take care of her for me?

She'll bring her charms to gladden you, and shall her stay
    be brief,
You'll have her lovely memories as solace for your grief,
I cannot promise she will stay, since all from Earth return,
But there are lessons, taught down there, I want this child
    to learn.

I've looked the wide world over in my search for teachers
    true,
And from the throngs that crowd life's lanes, I have
    selected you.

Now will you give her all your love nor think the labor
    vain,
Nor hate me when I come to call to take her back again?

I fancied that I heard them say, Dear Lord, Thy will be
   done!
For all the joy Thy child shall bring, the risk of grief we'll
   run.
We'll shelter her with tenderness, we'll love her while we
   may,
And for the happiness we've known forever grateful stay;
But shall the angels call for her much sooner than we've
   planned,
We'll brave the bitter grief that comes and try to understand.

Edgar Guest

She Was Waiting

*P*atience *is a bitter plant, but it has sweet fruit.*

German Proverb

I loved you when you were just an idea, just a dream of future motherhood. I loved planning, wondering what you would look like. It was hard to imagine holding your tiny body, actually creating a little person. Yet I knew that someday you would become a reality, someday my dream of becoming a mother would come true.

When that day came I felt I was dreaming. I couldn't believe you actually were. I rubbed my tummy and talked to you. I thought about your due date, the day that I would actually be able to look at you and hold you, to finally see what you look like, my little child. Everything I did, I did for you. Everything I ate, every meal I made, I thought of you, the tiny life that I was feeding.

Your daddy and I planned your room, we picked out names, we started a savings for your future. We already loved you. We couldn't wait to feel your miniature fingers squeezing our own. We looked forward to bathing your soft body, hearing your needy cries for us to nurture you.

We looked forward to your first steps, your first words, your first day at school. We yearned to help you with your homework and to go to your baseball games. It was hard for me to imagine my little child calling the man I love "Daddy." These are the small things we saw in the future during those months that you were growing inside me. We loved you!

In one minute these dreams were taken from us. On a foggy morning at a routine ultrasound, we found out that you had stopped growing weeks before. You had, in fact, left us without us ever knowing it. All our thoughts and dreams for you had been in vain. But we still loved you! It took a long time to get over this shock. We were told that I could be pregnant again in only a few months. But we wanted *you!*

Eventually we realized that God hadn't meant for us to have a child yet, that we would be more ready when it was meant to be. This comforted us, although we missed you. We had been excited about your arrival, but we could wait if it was meant to be. And we knew that when you did come, I would stay home with you and you would have had a better life, for your daddy would be able to finish school first. In this way, we finally accepted our loss.

It has been four years since that terrible loss. This morning, I sat in our wading pool with my three-year-old daughter. As I watched her tiny hands picking up scoops of water with her bucket, I marveled at her beautiful innocence. It truly was a miracle that we could be part of such a creation. Suddenly she looked at me very intently, and with a twinkle in her eye, she said, "Mommy, you weren't ready for me the first time I came, were you?" I put my arms around my wonderful daughter, and through my tears I could only say, "No, but we missed you very much while you were gone." We no longer have to mourn for our lost baby, for now I know that she has come back to us. This is the same child that we had fallen in love with so many years ago.

Sara Parker

6

A MATTER OF PERSPECTIVE

Two men look out through the same bars; one sees mud, and one the stars.

Frederick Langbridge

A Little off the Top, and a
Lesson to Remember

To be able to look back upon one's past life with satisfaction is to live twice.

Martial

Haircuts are part of military life. In the last 10 years, I plopped myself into that big chair at least 250 times. You might think that getting a haircut would become commonplace, a non-event, each barber blurring into the last. They don't, however, because of one very special haircut that I got 10 years ago.

In June of 1985, I was preparing to be commissioned as a second lieutenant through ROTC at Northeastern University in Boston. The ceremony was on a Saturday, leaving me just Sunday to make the drive to Fort Bragg, North Carolina, where I was due to report in first thing Monday morning. On Friday, I headed for the barbershop, having waited until the last minute so that my haircut would still look its sharpest not only on the big day, but on Monday. I was shocked, and momentarily panicked, to find that my regular barber of 15 years had chosen this day to start his long weekend. I knew where there was another shop, although I'd never patronized it. I drove across town and went inside.

There were no other customers. The barber sat in his own chair, reading the paper, but he popped up with a grin when I entered. He was a spry little man, olive-skinned, his own hair mostly absent on top. A thin mustache ran along his upper lip, well into the process of turning from black to gray. "You're next!" he said loudly, as though I might not have known it otherwise. He slapped his hand hard on the cracking leather seat, which was warm. He'd apparently been reading undisturbed for quite a while, which I took as a bad sign. He shook out the covering sheet with a snap before he draped it over me.

"What'll it be, my friend?"

"A nice, short taper, please. Keep the back and sides pretty close, but leave a little more on top. Not enough to have to part, though, okay?" I was unhappy, to say the least. My "real" barber wouldn't have had to ask, and I wouldn't have had to worry. I was getting the most important haircut of my life, the one I would be wearing when I reported for duty in less than 72 hours, and I was having to explain it to a guy who probably hadn't cut anyone's hair this short since the 1960s.

"You got it, no problem," he said, changing blades on his clippers. "No problem at all. You must be in the Army, or the Marines or something, huh?"

"Army," I replied curtly. I wasn't ever going to see this guy again, and I wasn't worried about making friends. But there was no stopping this happy guy. He acted like that was one question down and 19 more to go.

"You coming off of leave?" No time for me to answer. "You stationed up at Fort Devens, or where?" The clipper blade was warm against the side of my head and I could tell by the way it felt that at least he was taking it down short enough. I could have answered him a couple of ways, or even not answered at all, but not wanting to talk is not the same thing as wanting to be rude.

I said, "Actually I'm not stationed anywhere yet, but by Sunday I'll be reporting in at Fort Bragg, North Carolina. I'm being commissioned tomorrow morning at Faneuil Hall."

"Oh, ho!" he bellowed, and I was instantly sorry that I'd decided to speak. "Well, what do you know—a shave-tail. Boy, do I remember you guys! Always catching me doing something I wasn't supposed to. I was in the Army for a few years myself, you know, during World War II. Went through a lot of lieutenants, so I know. There's nothing worse than a brand new shave-tail, I'll tell you. No offense."

I wanted to bolt, right then and there, no matter what my hair looked like. I couldn't believe what I'd gotten myself into; trapped in the chair by some career-private with an ax to grind against officers. I knew that I was in for at least 10 more minutes of stories about how the trouble was never his fault, and how his officers wouldn't ever listen, always got lost and generally did everything wrong. I steeled myself for the inevitable.

"So you're being commissioned tomorrow, what do you know. That's something. Who's going to pin on your bars, your folks, right?" I nodded, hoping to keep the grilling as painless as possible. "They got a general or something coming to talk to you, I imagine."

That caught me off guard, and I answered with more than just a nod. What happened next, because of my answer to that simple question, forever changed the way I look at strangers. It made such an impression on me that I'm seeing it all again as I write this, 10 years later. "As a matter of fact," I replied, "General Tuck is coming down from Fort Devens to give us a pep talk and hand out commissions."

"Hey, I know him," the barber exclaimed, stopping his work. "Sure. General Tuck, he's a one-star, right? I met him just a couple of weeks ago."

"*You* did?" The emphasis was on the first word, sounding ruder than I meant it, but I couldn't possibly imagine why this guy would be meeting a general.

"Yeah, I sure did. I had to go up to Fort Devens. Here, let me show you what I got." He set the clippers down and pulled open a drawer under the mirror. He pulled out a small blue box, which I had not then the experience to recognize, and thrust it at me. "Here, take a look."

Bronze Star Medal, read the gold letters on the box. I opened the box, revealing the medal nestled inside. I looked up sharply at the barber, and he handed me a certificate. I read it quickly, feeling smaller and smaller as I did so.

In February 1945, an American rifle platoon was stalled in its attempt to capture a small German town with a long German name. The soldiers were nearly out of ammunition and night was falling. If not resupplied, they would have to withdraw, giving up ground they would have to retake. Corporal Dominic Cerutti volunteered to go back and get more ammunition. Leading two men, he crawled back across the ground that was exposed to enemy fire and hustled to the company's headquarters. Returning in the darkness through contested territory, he led his party directly to the platoon's position, bringing with him enough ammunition to hold on through the night. Although the party was fired upon by the enemy, because of Corporal Cerutti's leadership, no one was injured. For his bravery in performing this duty, Corporal Cerutti was awarded the Bronze Star Medal for Valor.

I looked at Corporal Cerutti, 40 years older . . . Barber Cerutti now, and all I could say was "Wow." He held the medal in his own hands now, gazing at it with obvious pride, but also, it seemed to me, with pain. "And you're just getting this now?" I asked softly.

"Yeah, well they told me that I'd got it when I was getting ready to come home, but nobody could find any orders or anything. I wasn't about to wait around, so I came back without it, and, of course, when I got to the States nobody knew anything about it. I didn't have time to worry about it then, you know, because I had my wife and a kid to take care of. I had to get some work. And right then, at that time, I probably didn't care much. Just glad it was all over."

Forty years later, his son-in-law cared enough to contact the Army and see that the medal was awarded.

Dominic Cerutti hadn't cared much. He had done his job as best he could, he had come home when it was done, and that was what mattered, not the credit or recognition. I decided right there that this was a good lesson to take with me into active duty.

But there is another lesson here, and fortunately, I learned this one as well. Many of us in the military are quick to judge the people that we meet by the badges and patches on their uniforms, just as in civilian life, we may base our assessments of a stranger's character on his or her clothes, car or salary. We forget that everyone has talents and achievements in their past that may not be immediately visible in the present. The fact is that people are a lot like icebergs; there's always so much more under the surface.

I had forgotten this important rule that day, but I have always remembered it since. I had entered the shop of a nameless and faceless barber, only to find myself meeting a genuine hero.

Andy Entwistle

The Scar

A little boy invited his mother to attend his elementary school's first teacher-parent conference. To the little boy's dismay, she said she would go. This would be the first time that his classmates and teacher met his mother and he was embarrassed by her appearance. Although she was a beautiful woman, there was a severe scar that covered nearly the entire right side of her face. The boy never wanted to talk about why or how she got the scar.

At the conference, the people were impressed by the kindness and natural beauty of his mother despite the scar, but the little boy was still embarrassed and hid himself from everyone. He did, however, get within earshot of a conversation between his mother and his teacher, and heard them speaking.

"How did you get the scar on your face?" the teacher asked.

The mother replied, "When my son was a baby, he was in a room that caught on fire. Everyone was too afraid to go in because the fire was out of control, so I went in. As I was running toward his crib, I saw a beam coming down and I placed myself over him trying to shield him. I was knocked unconscious but fortunately, a fireman came in and saved both of us." She touched the burned side of her face. "This scar will be permanent, but to this day, I have never regretted doing what I did."

At this point, the little boy came out running toward his mother with tears in his eyes. He hugged her and felt an overwhelming sense of the sacrifice that his mother had made for him. He held her hand tightly for the rest of the day.

Lih Yuh Kuo

Thelma

Humor is mankind's greatest blessing.

Mark Twain

Even at the age of 75, Thelma was very vivacious and full of life. When her husband passed away, her children suggested that she move to a "senior living community." A gregarious and life-loving person, Thelma decided to do so.

Shortly after moving in, Thelma became a self-appointed activities director, coordinating all sorts of things for the people in the community to do and quickly became very popular and made many friends.

When Thelma turned 80, her newfound friends showed their appreciation by throwing a surprise birthday party for her. When Thelma entered the dining room for dinner that night, she was greeted by a standing ovation and one of the coordinators led her to the head table. The night was filled with laughter and entertainment, but throughout the evening, Thelma could not take her eyes off a gentleman sitting at the other end of the table.

When the festivities ended, Thelma quickly rose from her seat and rushed over to the man. "Pardon me," Thelma said. "Please forgive me if I made you feel uncomfortable by staring at you all night. I just couldn't help myself from looking your way. You see, you look just like my fifth husband."

"Your fifth husband!" replied the gentleman. "Forgive me for asking, but how many times have you been married?"

With that, a smile came across Thelma's face as she responded, "Four."

They were married shortly after.

Shari Smith

Through the Eyes of a Child

After a holiday break, the teacher asked her small pupils how they spent their holiday. One little boy's reply went like this:

We always spend Christmas with Granma and Granpa. They used to live up here in a big brick house but Granpa got retarded and they moved to Florida. They live in a park with a lot of other retarded people. They all live in tin huts and ride tricycles that are too big for me.

They all go to a building they call the wrecked hall, but it is fixed now. They all play a game with big checkers and push them around on the floor with sticks. There is a swimming pool but I guess nobody teaches them; they just stand there in the water with their hats on.

My Granma used to bake cookies for me, but nobody cooks there. They all go to restaurants that are fast and have discounts. When you come to the park, there is a dollhouse with a man sitting in it. He watches all day so they can't get out without him seeing them. I guess everybody forgets who they are because they all wear badges with their names on them.

Granma says that Granpa worked hard all his life to earn his retardment.

I wish they would move back home, but I guess the man in the dollhouse won't let them out.

Author Unknown

To Save a Life

*It's good to remember that we aren't helpless.
There is always something we can do.*

Carla Gorrell

In those chaotic years of the late 1940s, just after World War II ended, an immigrant family in New York tried to contact their surviving relatives in Hungary. Communications were sporadic, the mails untrustworthy, records destroyed or inaccurate or lost. It could take many weeks or months for letters to travel to Europe and find their way to recipients and just as long for replies to return. Reliable information was hard, if not impossible, to get.

The immigrant family wondered if their relatives were still alive. Had they all survived the war? Where were they living? It was so hard to tell. Then, they received a letter, in Hungarian, from Uncle Lazlo in a small town near Budapest. Yes, some of the family had survived the war. The letter was tantalizingly incomplete in the news it offered. But it was clear that they were hungry and hurting. Food and other necessities were in very short supply. The black market was operating in full force, the currency was inflated and nearly valueless. It took all their energy and wit to survive each day.

The New Yorkers were appalled at the story of devastation and deprivation they could piece together by reading and rereading this crumpled letter, written on the tissue-thin paper of the airmail of that time. Grateful to be able to read again in Hungarian, the older members of the family translated for their American-born children. They argued about the translation of this phrase or that. But it was clear that they could be useful to their far-off family.

They determined to send survival supplies to their cousins, aunts and uncles. They tried to imagine what would be needed and appreciated, but, not having directly experienced war themselves, it was not easy to come up with a list of things to send. They included canned meats and vegetables and chocolates. Necessities like toilet paper and bandages made the final list, too. In the end, the package grew to several cartons, stuffed to the brim with many items. Little spaces in each carton were filled with whatever odds and ends were at hand: candies, handkerchiefs, writing paper and pencils.

At last, the cartons were sealed and painstakingly wrapped with brown paper and stout string to help endure the long and chancy journey overseas. Brought to the post office, the cartons began their journey undramatically.

And that is all the New York family heard for months and months. They wondered if the packages had gone astray or been stolen. Had something terrible happened to their family in the confusion of post-war Europe? What irony it would be to have survived the war itself and be killed or injured in its aftermath. The family worried. At every dinner, at every gathering, the talk circled around the packages and the family in Europe.

One uncle, sitting at the table at Thanksgiving dinner, recriminated, "You should have included money for postage! Perhaps they can't afford to write us!" He was met with angry stares. "Well, I don't care what you think, I am going to send them some money for postage."

"Better you should send enough money for them to come over here!" someone retorted.

"Big shot!" he replied. "It's easy for you to spend the money I don't have, isn't it? Listen, there are quotas for immigration. It's not that easy to get on the list for America, money or not."

"Maybe we didn't send the right things they needed," someone else contributed. The discussion continued, back and forth. The content was unimportant. They were just expressing, again and again, their worry and concern and their feeling of helplessness. How could they really help?

The silence from their distant family was depressing, especially in the light of the newsreels they saw at the theater (television being very uncommon then) showing emaciated Europeans walking dispiritedly through rubble-strewn streets, dodging bomb craters or being deloused in long lines by GI medics. Headlines fueled their worries as newspapers wrote about the Marshall Plan and the need for much help in rebuilding war-ravaged countries. Stories circulated about people starving to death. News of an historically severe winter in Europe and shortages of food and fuel upset the family even more.

Although far from wealthy, the family sent more packages, almost every week, off into the void, unsure as to whether or not they were received by their loved ones. More silence ensued. It was maddening.

Finally, another letter arrived from Uncle Lazlo. It had been bent, wrinkled and torn at the edges, but it was still readable.

"My Dearest Cousin," the letter began formally, as Uncle Lazlo was in the habit of writing. "We are in receipt of three packages you sent us.

"We are forever in your debt for these good things. You cannot know how timely was their arrival. Food is so scarce here and Anna was sick all the time with fevers. This food has meant everything to us. I must confess that we sold some of the things you sent us on the black market in order to get money for our rent." The letter went on to discuss almost every item in the cartons and the uses to which they had been put. Then came a mystery.

"We also cannot ever thank you enough for the medicine you sent. It is so difficult to get any medicine at all and often it is of poor potency and doesn't work at all. Cousin Gesher has been in continuous pain for several years and your medicine has miraculously cured him! He was walking only with the help of a cane. His knees were so swollen. These medicines make him almost normal again. My back pain is completely gone as are Lizabeta's headaches.

"America is great and its science is great. You must send more of that medicine as it is nearly used up.

"Again, thank you. We love you all and pray for when we might see you once more."

The family read and reread Uncle Lazlo's letter. What medicine did we send? They racked their brains to recall but, shamefacedly, had to admit to each other that they had omitted sending any medicines at all! What was Uncle Lazlo talking about? Was some medicine accidentally included? If so, what was it? After all, they needed to send some more right away. The mystery couldn't be solved. A letter was drafted to Uncle Lazlo asking him to provide the name of the medicine he so urgently required. The envelope was brought to the post office. The clerk was asked for advice on how to send the letter by the fastest route possible. There was, at the time, nothing faster than regular air mail, express services being as yet only a dream. He did suggest including an international postal reply coupon which would pay for return postage and that was done.

The family waited again, relieved that their packages had been of help but puzzled by the "mystery of the unknown medicines." Two months passed and then another letter arrived.

"My Dearest Cousins," began Uncle Lazlo, "we are grateful to have heard from you again. Since the first three packages, another two have arrived, and then your letter. Again, you sent that wonderful medicine. It did not come with instructions for use but we are guessing on the dosage. And translating from English to Hungarian is very difficult for us since only young Sandor has studied it in school. Lucky for us he could translate the name of the medicine. It is 'Life Savers.' Please send more as soon as you can. Love, Lazlo."

The filler, in several cartons, had been rolls of that well-known American candy, Life Savers. A literal translation transformed America's favorite candy into a source of great hope.

Hanoch McCarty

The Baby Flight

I had never held a deformed infant in my arms before.

In fact, I had never even seen a deformed infant before. Now I found myself delivering three tiny orphans to their adoptive parents on Christmas Eve.

I taught English in Korea. College students rioted and succeeded in closing the college where I taught. Fed up, I desired to go home. A friend informed me of the "baby flights," a program whereby one can travel from Korea to the U.S. dirt cheap. But there was a hitch. The traveler must transport *three* orphans. The alternative was to pay the full fare.

I found myself boarding a plane with three infants, aged 3 months, 7 months and 18 months. They came with runny noses, wet diapers and colds. As the plane took off, the poor kids howled. The plane vibrated violently and all the babies quieted. Seconds later, the plane stopped shaking and in unison the babies howled. The passengers burst into laughter.

One thing disturbed me. One of the infants was a deformed dwarf. Her massive head with disproportionately minute arms and fingers shocked me. I wondered if her new parents realized what they had coming. But the one on my lap was wet and the milk formula was low. I rapidly learned how to clean a wet bottom, put on a new diaper and stick a pacifier in an open mouth.

Two American soldiers asked if they could each hold a baby.

"No problem," I said and they both walked off with a baby.

I sat there holding the baby with the very large head. She blinked her long gorgeous eyelashes and smiled. Funny how things like that can change you. From that point on she radiated beauty, and never left my arms.

Before landing in Tokyo, the soldiers handed back the babies. I clung onto *my* baby and one at a time changed the diapers of the two babies the soldiers had just handed me. As I pulled off their clothes, single dollar bills fell to the floor. I glanced at the departing soldiers. One of them blurted, "Little buggers are gonna need all the cash they can get. Merry Christmas!"

By now I had developed a strong bond with my baby. I even named her Tina. The more I thought about giving her to someone else the more I worried about her prospective parents.

While waiting in the terminal I noticed a young attractive Asian woman pacing back and forth near me. She stared at the babies and me and then walked off. Finally she spun around and confronted me, "Are they orphans?"

"Yes," I replied.

"I was one of them 24 years ago. May I hold one?"

The lovely woman took the noisiest one of the lot. She carried the child on the plane for the next leg of our journey, and she cared for the infant for the rest of the flight. Occasionally she'd show up and lend a hand feeding or changing the others when she could. After two more stops and a total of 27 hours, the plane landed. New parents rushed in and sped off with two of the babies. I still held Tina and it seemed like nobody was coming on board for her. Worried that no one wanted her I trudged off the plane. Then I saw them and stopped, unable to move. Little hands of a dwarf couple reached up to me.

As I passed Tina down to them, she said "Oma" to me. That means mom in Korean. At that point, I sat and cried.

I watched the delighted tiny family walk off to a new life and thought, "How perfect."

But the next year I paid the full fare. The baby flight was too expensive.

Paul Karrer

How to Tell When You're Rich

*What we steadily, consciously, habitually think
we are, that we tend to become.*

Ann Landers

When I was a kid in Minnesota, watermelon was a delicacy. One of my father's buddies, Bernie, was a prosperous fruit-and-vegetable wholesaler, who operated a warehouse in St. Paul.

Every summer, when the first watermelons rolled in, Bernie would call. Dad and I would go to Bernie's warehouse and take up our positions. We'd sit on the edge of the dock, feet dangling, and lean over, minimizing the volume of juice we were about to spill on ourselves.

Bernie would take his machete, crack our first watermelon, hand us both a big piece and sit down next to us. Then we'd bury our faces in watermelon, eating only the heart—the reddest, juiciest, firmest, most seed-free, most perfect part—and throw away the rest.

Bernie was my father's idea of a rich man. I always thought it was because he was such a successful businessman. Years later, I realized that what my father admired about Bernie's wealth was less its substance than its application. Bernie knew how to stop working, get together with friends and eat only the heart of the watermelon.

What I learned from Bernie is that being rich is a state of mind. Some of us, no matter how much money we have, will never be free enough to eat only the heart of the watermelon. Others are rich without ever being more than a paycheck ahead.

If you don't take the time to dangle your feet over the dock and chomp into life's small pleasures, your career is probably overwhelming your life.

For many years, I forgot that lesson I'd learned as a kid on the loading dock. I was too busy making all the money I could.

Well, I've relearned it. I hope I have time left to enjoy the accomplishments of others and to take pleasure in the day. That's the heart of the watermelon. I have learned again to throw the rest away.

Finally, I am rich.

Harvey Mackay

Chuck

Earth is crammed with heaven.

Elizabeth Barrett Browning

I hate shopping for groceries. I treat it like running a marathon through the aisles, and I pride myself on using the same seasoned check-out personnel to ensure a hasty retreat from the insanity during the holiday seasons. Don't get me wrong, I am a Christmas-aholic! I just hate grocery shopping!

Imagine my dismay when I picked one of the "wrong lines" that was 10 deep with overstuffed carts. My temper rose when all of the other lines seemed to be inching toward the cashier and ours was at a standstill. Echoes of "What's the problem?" and "Why are we putting up with this?" erupted from our conga line.

Upon closer inspection, I discovered that the culprit behind the delay was Chuck, the sacker. He talked to each and every item as he gently placed it into the sack, "Oh, Mr. Cake Mix, you are going to become a Christmas dessert for someone special. Hello, Mr. Cereal, you are going to make the boys and girls grow up nice and healthy," etc. After all of the items were sacked and ready to go he would look at the customer and say, "I know your family loves you because you take such good care of them. Merry Christmas!" Did I shut up and wait my turn!

Chuck helped me take everything to my car and I tipped him $2. He looked at the two dollar bills; he looked at me. Then his face lit up, and he jumped in the air and yelled at the top of his lungs, "Look at me, look at me! Someone thinks I'm worth two whole dollars!" as he danced his way back into the store.

The next time I went to the store, one of the employees said she had witnessed that particular day's events. She said, "Thanks for giving Chuck a tip. We know he has value, but it is far more important for Chuck to know he has value."

I replied, "No, I have to thank him for reminding me of the true Christmas spirit and for teaching me this price-less lesson."

Petey Parker

Calling On a Girl Named Becky

"May I help you?" the man behind the counter at the ceramic shop asked. I barely heard him. My gaze was trans-fixed by the pretty teenager perched on the stool beside him. Her curly brown hair, round rosy cheeks and shim-mering green eyes were so distantly familiar. Once upon a time, eyes like those had captured a schoolboy's heart.

In the summer of 1973, Becky came to work as a wait-ress at my family's quaint stone inn in the mountains of North Carolina. She burst through the swinging kitchen doors one June morning just as I was sitting down to breakfast. It was love at first sight.

Becky was 16. I was 11. She was pretty, vivacious and outgoing. I was shy, a little on the pudgy side, and, heretofore, more inclined toward bullfrogs and tree climb-ing than creatures of the fairer sex.

But there was something about Becky. The certain way she tossed back her head whenever an unwelcome curl drifted down over her eye. Her habit of chewing on the nail of her pinkie finger when she was lost in thought. The way she gracefully tucked her pencil behind her ear after taking an order. Becky was no garden-variety girl.

"What's that?" Becky would ask innocently, pointing to some imaginary speck just south of my Adam's apple. I always fell for it, and she relished bringing her finger up to pop me on the chin when I looked down. "Gotcha 'gain," she'd say grinning.

The summer of '73 Becky gave me a boy's greatest keepsake—attention. She was never too busy to share a secret, a joke or a playful flick of a wet dish towel. In return, I cleaned off her tables, fetched her soft drinks, sneaked her extra desserts and worshiped the ground she walked on.

"I think he's cute," Becky whispered one afternoon just loud enough for me to overhear. "Especially when he blushes."

"Becky, I love you," I boldly ventured one morning into the bathroom mirror. "I'll love you till the end of time."

Unfortunately, our time was sliding by like a well-waxed shuffleboard disk and there was nothing I could do to slow it.

"Robbie, can I talk to you for a minute?" Becky asked one stormy August afternoon. My heart was racing. What could she want? Would she finally confirm her love for me?

"I'm going back to school soon," she announced. "I won't be around much anymore." I swallowed hard. "You've been a great friend," she said quietly. "I'll miss you very much."

I struggled to stay composed. I had worked so hard for her to see me as a grown-up and I didn't want to fall apart now. But when she grew blurry and my chin began to quiver, I knew there was no turning back.

"I love you," I said abruptly and then cried my eyes out.

For a few minutes she watched me—a bit startled by my sudden sobbing confession. Then she gently took my hand.

"Robbie," she spoke softly. "I think you're very special and I love you so much as my friend. But I'm not the one for you, and I think, deep down, you know that."

Slowly, like a steam engine pulling into the station, my sobbing ground to a halt.

Becky smiled at me until she forced me to smile back. "Someday," she confided, "you're going to find a girl so wonderful you'll know she's the right one for you. Then, you'll forget all about me. I promise you."

"May I help you," the ceramic-shop man repeated a bit more firmly. "Is Becky in?" I muttered finally. "Are you a friend of hers?" he shot back suspiciously.

"Sort of," I mumbled. "About 20 years ago she spent the summer waiting tables at my family's inn. My father and I were waxing nostalgic last evening, and her name came up. He said I might be able to find her here."

His furrowed brow softened and he extended his hand. "I'm her husband. This here's her daughter." The girl snatched the phone from the wall and began dialing. "Becky's at home today," the man explained. "She's not been well."

"Momma, somebody here knows you." The girl spoke in her customary mountain twang. "He says you used to work at his family's inn." She listened for a moment and then wordlessly handed me the phone.

I stared at it in my hand as if holding one for the first time. She smiled a dimpled smile that seemed to say, "Go ahead."

"Hi Becky," I stammered a bit too energetically. The other end of the line was completely still. Five seconds. Ten.

"Robbie, is that you?" The voice I knew. It was deeper, more grown-up—but unforgettable.

"It's me," I assured her.

"Well, how have you been?" she asked with a smile in her voice.

"Fine, Becky. How about you?"

We reminisced—small talk among long-lost friends trying to fold 20 years into a five-minute phone conversation.

"I have such happy memories of that summer," Becky said at last. "I am so touched you remembered. I only wish I could be there to see you because you really made my year."

"But, Becky," I said smiling at the girl across the counter, "I'm looking at you right now."

"Now, don't you go and fall in love with my daughter," she teased.

My cheeks flushed bright red. I was 11 again.

Robert Tate Miller

A MATTER OF PERSPECTIVE

Innocence Abroad

Fate loves the fearless.

James Russell Lowell

My wife prepared breakfast as I stood at the dining room window gazing beyond a sentinel row of palm trees at the early morning sun forcing its rays through wisps of Texas fog. Our three-year-old daughter, Becky, was in the backyard, her attention riveted to the antics of a pair of quarreling blue jays.

Suddenly I snapped to attention. An awesome creature, ugly and misshapen, was meandering up the alley. In the hazy light of the early morning, it appeared like a monster out of the past. It was a huge thing, armed with long, curving tusks; down its high, arched back ran a great ridge, crowned with stiff bristles. I realized suddenly what it was: a pugnacious javelina, the fierce, wild hog of the Southwest plains country.

I took no time to ponder where it came from or how it had managed to penetrate a thickly populated residential section, for it was progressing slowly, grunting, sniffing and rooting with its long snout as it ambled along. I started to shout to Becky to run inside, but I was too late. She and the animal had sighted each other simultaneously. The grunting shifted to a low, menacing rumble. The tip of the long nose was an inch from the ground, gleaming button eyes were fastened on my daughter, the beast's four stubby legs were braced to charge.

I started to dash upstairs for a gun, but I knew I could never get it in time. As though hypnotized, I stared at the drama that was unfolding just a few yards away.

Becky approached the javelina, hands outstretched, making gurgling childish sounds as she advanced. The hog stood its ground, its grunts even more threatening. I looked at those fearsome tusks and the sharp even teeth—one slash could lay a man open.

I started to call to my wife, but something held me mute. If she should look out the window and scream, a chain reaction might be touched off that could end in terrible tragedy.

Becky, who had been only a few steps away from the beast when they first sighted each other, closed the distance between them with calm deliberation. With hands still outstretched, she reached the side of the beast. One small hand went up to a tough, bristly ear and scratched it. The deep-throated rumblings gradually turned into a gravely, almost purring sound. I thought irrelevantly of the idling of a powerful motor. The top of the round, wet nose was gently nudging against Becky's ankle. Unbelievably, the animal seemed to be enjoying the attention he was receiving, and my pulse beat slowly dropped to normal. Some perception within the ugly creature must have told him that he had nothing to fear from this tiny child.

The encounter ended as abruptly as it began. Becky suddenly turned away and came toward the house. The javelina seemed to realize that the short love fest was over and slowly ambled on its way.

Becky passed me as she came through the room. "Nice doggie, Daddy," she said nonchalantly.

Henry N. Ferguson

Looking Down

Up there you go around every hour and a half; time after time, after time, and you wake up in the morning over the mid-East, and over North Africa. You look out of your window as you're eating breakfast—and there's the whole Mediterranean area, and Greece and Rome, and the Sinai and Israel. And you realize that what you are seeing in one glance was the whole history of man for centuries; the cradle of civilization.

You go across the Atlantic Ocean, back across North Africa. You do it again and again. You identify with Houston, and then you identify with Los Angeles, and Phoenix and New Orleans. And the next thing you know, you are starting to identify with North Africa. You look forward to it. You anticipate it. And the whole process of what you identify with begins to shift.

When you go around it every hour and a half, you begin to recognize that your identity is with that whole thing. And that makes a very powerful change inside of you . . .

As you look down you can't imagine how many borders and boundaries you cross—again and again. And you can't even see them. But you know that in the "wake-up" scene you saw before over the Mid-East, there are thousands of people fighting over some imaginary line that you can't even see. And you wish you could take each of them hand in hand, and say "Look at that! Look at that! What's important?"

Later the person sitting next to you goes out to the moon. And he sees the Earth, not as something big with all kinds of beautiful details; he sees it as a small thing out there. And the contrast between that small blue and white Christmas tree ornament and that black sky really comes through . . . and you realize that on that little blue and white spot is everything that means anything to you—all history, and music, and war, and death, and birth, and love, and tears, and joy—all of it on that little blue and white spot that you can cover with your thumb.

It comes through to you so clearly that you are a sensing point for man. You look down and you see the surface of the globe that you have lived on all this time and you know that all those people down there—they are you. And somehow, you represent them and have a responsibility to them. Somehow you recognize that you are a piece of this total life. You're out there on the forefront and you have to bring your experience back somehow. It becomes a rather special responsibility, and it tells you about your relationship to this thing we call the world.

All through this I've used the word "you" because it's not me, Rusty Schweickart . . . or any of the others that have had this experience. It's not just my problem—my challenge—my joy to integrate into daily life. It's everyone's.

Rusty Schweickart

7

OVERCOMING OBSTACLES

I'm not afraid of storms, for I'm learning how to sail my ship.

Louisa May Alcott

Angel at Work

I thank God for my handicaps, for through them I have found myself, my work and my God.

Helen Keller

An envelope addressed to me in unusually beautiful type-script caught my eye as I sorted through the day's mail which was piled high on my desk. Something about the letter commanded my attention, so I opened it first.

The same beautiful type-script in ephemeral light-brown unfolded in balanced precision across the sheet of expensive stationery. The entire letter was a model of perfection for personal correspondence. It invited me to read it:

Dear Dr. Curtis:

I have been thrilled by your talks at the Sunday Services of the Science of Mind Church at the Fox Wilshire Theatre during the past month. I get so much out of them. Your lessons should be published so that everyone can be inspired by them as I am.

Here is a suggestion. If you will send me the tape recording of your Sunday talk each week, I will transcribe it for you and return the tape along with the typed transcription.

I pray that you will allow me to be of service in this way. I want to help others share the great good which you have given me. Just have your secretary call and someone will pick up the tape each Monday morning.

God is blessing you and your great work.

Sincerely yours,

Mary Louise Zollars

The signature was typed in the same unusual typescript. There was no handwriting.

As I finished the letter, I experienced the exultation that always accompanies answered prayer. For months I had been looking for someone to transcribe my Sunday sermons, but could find no one who would transcribe directly from the tape I used on my cumbersome tape recorder. A start-stop mechanism had not yet been invented and operating the recorder by hand and typing at the same time was just too much to handle. In the meantime, I was frustrated as the tape recordings piled up. I had no transcriptions upon which to base a book.

And now, out of the blue, came this letter from Mary Louise Zollars. I hastened to call the number given in the letter and asked to speak to her.

"I would be happy to give her a message," a friendly feminine voice replied.

"May I speak to her personally?" I asked.

"She can't come to the phone right now," the voice replied. "Please give me your message."

"Thank you," I said, "Just tell her Donald Curtis called in response to her wonderful letter."

"She will be glad you called," was the answer. "Could you tell me when someone can pick up the tape of your Sunday lesson?"

"I would be happy to deliver it personally," I persisted. I was eager to have personal contact with this angel who had been sent to me.

"That won't be necessary. Please have the tape ready at your office at noon tomorrow, and it will be picked up. Oh—Miss Zollars has her own tape recorder to play the tape on for her to transcribe. The tape and the transcription will be returned to you before the end of the week."

"Thank you very much," I replied. "The tape will be at my office tomorrow as you have requested."

I was puzzled by the seeming mystery of the arrangement, but I gladly went along with it because of the great good fortune that had come to me.

Two days later the first tape and the pages of the transcription were returned to my office. They were in the same unusual type-script and light brown ink, and each page was perfect. The spaces were consistent, the margins justified, and there wasn't a typo anywhere. I was elated as I read through the manuscript. This was exactly what I needed for the first draft of my book. I hastened to call Miss Zollars to thank her. The same friendly voice answered the phone.

"Hello," I spoke. "This is Donald Curtis. Could I speak to Miss Zollars? I want to thank her for the beautiful transcription."

"Oh, hello, Dr. Curtis," came the answer. "I will give Miss Zollars your message. She will be glad you called. Remember, be sure to have the tape of your Sunday talk available at your office on Monday morning. We'll pick it up as before."

This same procedure went on for nearly a year. The flow of perfectly typed transcriptions continued to reach me each week, and I gleaned enough good "stuff" from them to complete my first book. But I still had no personal contact with my transcribing angel. She didn't answer my phone calls, but answered my "thank you" letters with warm letters of her own, all written perfectly in the same unique style.

A personal call came for me one afternoon, and a familiar voice greeted me, "Dr. Curtis, I am calling for Miss Zollars. She would like to invite you to tea this afternoon at five. Can you come?"

I answered in the affirmative, and at five o'clock sharp I presented myself at the address given. I was greeted by a pleasant matronly lady whose voice I immediately recognized. "Good afternoon, Dr. Curtis. How good of you to come. Miss Zollars is waiting for you in her sitting room."

I was ushered into a warm, pleasant room where a young woman sat in a wheelchair, her head twisted to one side in a grimace, and her body twitching as her hands were held firmly between her knees. Her face lit up as she endeavored to smile and speak. The entire experience was painful to behold, but joy and light radiated from Mary Louise.

Side by side on a raised platform in front of her wheelchair were a large tape recorder and an old-fashioned manual typewriter. Following our greeting, Mary Louise started the tape recorder with the toes of one foot, let it play for a moment, and then typed the passage with her toes on the typewriter, before repeating the process. She beamed with pride as she accomplished the entire process with her feet, holding her hands tightly between her knees to keep her arms from flailing.

Mary Louise had been spastic since birth, but overcame her handicap with an indomitable sense of humor and the skilled training of her feet. Her companion, friend and nurse-helper was the friendly lady whom I had gotten to know on the telephone. The two were inseparable and working together; their life was full and meaningful.

Mary Louise continued to transcribe my tapes for several years and never asked any reward except what she called the joy of doing it. On the thousands of pages of transcriptions that Mary Louise typed with her toes, I never found one error.

This remarkable lady has been one of my closest friends for many years, and is the most beautiful soul whom I have ever known. She continues to live a full, dedicated life of service, and seems completely untroubled by the fact that her every overt action is performed with her feet, reinforced by the ebullient humor which bubbles up from within her.

My life has been enriched and blessed by this angel who lives to help others.

Donald Curtis

Consider This

You never really lose until you quit trying.

Mike Ditka
NFL Football Coach

Consider this:

- Most people have no idea of the amount of practice, discipline and effort that goes into becoming a superstar. For example, former U.S. Senator and former New York Knicks basketball star Bill Bradley practiced relentlessly. He had five spots on the basketball court from which he would shoot 25 times. If he didn't hit 22 baskets out of 25 shots, he'd start over. He was determined to stay there and do it over and over until he could do it right almost every time.
- Novelist Carson McCullers endured three strokes before she was 29. While she was crippled, partially paralyzed and in constant pain, she suffered the profound shock of her husband's suicide. Others may have surrendered to such afflictions, but she settled for writing no less than a page a day. On that unrelenting

schedule she turned out many distinguished novels including *Member of the Wedding, The Ballad of the Sad Cafe* and *The Heart Is a Lonely Hunter.*

- When NFL running back Herschel Walker was in junior high school, he wanted to play football, but the coach told him he was too small. He advised young Herschel to go out for track instead. Undaunted by the lack of encouragement and support, he ignored the coach's advice and began an intensive training program to build himself up. Only a few years later, Herschel Walker won the Heisman trophy.

- Having a learning disability doesn't have to stop you. Consider the following people who did not let learning disabilities stop them from pursuing and achieving their dreams:

  John Lennon, singer, musician and songwriter.

  General George Patton, American general and tank commander.

  Bill Wilson, founder of Alcoholics Anonymous.

  Woodrow Wilson, 27th president of the United States.

  Harry Belafonte, singer, actor, producer, civil rights activist.

  George Burns, actor, comedian.

  Cher, singer, actress.

  Agatha Christie, British novelist.

  Winston Churchill, Prime Minister of Great Britain.

  Tom Cruise, actor.

  Leonardo da Vinci, artist and scientist.

  Albert Einstein, scientist.

  Whoopi Goldberg, actress and comedian.

- Physical disabilities do not have to stop you either. Consider these people with challenges and the tremendous levels of success they have achieved:

  John Milton, the famous poet and author, was blind.

Itzhak Perlman, world-class concert violinist, is paralyzed from the waist down.

James Thurber, cartoonist and humorist, was visually impaired.

Heather Whitestone, 1994 Miss America, is deaf.

Jim Eisenrich, professional baseball player, has Tourette's syndrome.

Rafer Johnson, the decathlon champion, was born with a club foot.

Stephen Hawking, a theoretical physicist and lecturer at Cambridge University and bestselling author of *A Brief History of Time*, has Lou Gehrig's disease.

James Earl Jones, world-renowned actor, stuttered from ages 6 to 14.

• Tom Dempsy was born without toes on his right foot. Although this might be considered a disability to some, he was born to a family who considered him quite capable and able-bodied. Because he focused on his vision of what he was capable of rather than his limitations, he eventually became a place kicker in the National Football League. While playing with the New Orleans Saints, he kicked one of the longest field goals—63 yards!—in NFL history. He achieved this feat with a kicking foot half the size of his other one.

If we did all the things we were capable of doing, we would literally astound ourselves.

Thomas Edison

• Marathoner Joan Benoit underwent knee surgery only 17 days before the U.S. Olympic trials, but her determination enabled her not only to make the team, but also to win the first ever Olympic gold medal in her event.

• King Camp Gillette dreamed of a cockeyed invention that caused investors, metal engineers and experts at MIT to snicker. They all believed that there was no way a razor could be made sharp enough to provide a clean shave and yet be cheap enough that it could be thrown away when it was dull. Gillette labored four years to produce the first disposable razor and another six years to get it placed on store shelves. Although only 51 blades sold during the first year, 90,844 were purchased in the second year and Gillette's risk-taking innovation was on its way to revolutionizing the shaving industry.

• Michelangelo endured seven long years of lying on his back on a scaffold to complete the painting of the Sistine Chapel.

• Eric Mohn has won numerous awards in local, national and even international art competitions for his watercolor paintings. Senator John Warner of Virginia and Senator Robert Byrd of West Virginia are two people who have bought his paintings in recent years. Remarkably, Mohn is paralyzed in all four limbs and paints with a brush held in his mouth. Another remarkable fact about his accomplishments is that Mohn never even pursued art as a hobby or career until 1977, 13 years after a car accident left him paralyzed from the chest down.

The human spirit cannot be paralyzed. If you are breathing, you can dream.

Mike Brown

• Dennis Walters was a promising young golfer when a freak golf cart accident paralyzed both of his legs. He had no intention of watching golf from the sidelines. Dennis learned how to hit golf balls from a sitting position, designed a swivel seat for his golf cart and eventually drove the ball 250 yards from a sitting position. Walters went on to become a golf instructor and a popular golf exhibitionist.

• Beethoven was completely deaf when he composed his masterpiece, the Ninth Symphony.

• Tom Sullivan lost his sight at birth because the wrong solution was put into his eyes. He later decided that he could play every sport but baseball, basketball and tennis. Today he golfs, swims, runs, skis, rides horses and enjoys life to the fullest.

• David W. Hartman went blind at the age of eight. His dream to become a medical doctor was thwarted by Temple University Medical School, when he was told that no one without eyesight had ever completed medical school. He courageously faced the challenge of "reading" medical books by having 25 complete medical textbooks audio-recorded for him. At 27, David Hartman became the first blind student to ever complete medical school.

• Almost no one at 3M believed that the Post-It notes had a future, but Art Fry kept handing them out to people until they gave the product a chance. Even after the first marketing attempt failed, Art did not give up on the idea. He persisted until the idea became a colossal success.

In the middle of every difficulty lies opportunity.

Albert Einstein

• Colonel Sanders had the construction of a new road put him out of business in 1967. He went to over 1,000 places trying to sell his chicken recipe before he found a buyer interested in his 11 herbs and spices. Seven years later, at the age of 75, Colonel Sanders sold his fried chicken company for a finger-lickin' $15 million!

• A young woman aspiring to land a permanent position in broadcasting found more failure than success. No United States radio station would give her an opportunity because "a woman wouldn't be able to attract an audience." She made her way to Puerto Rico and then, paying her own way, flew to the Dominican Republic to cover and sell her stories on the uprising there. Back in the States she valiantly pursued her passion, but after 18 firings, she wondered if a career in broadcasting was ever meant to be. Finally she persuaded an executive to hire her, but he wanted her to host a political talk show. She was familiar with the microphone but not politics. Using her comfortable conversational style, she talked about what the Fourth of July meant to her and invited callers to do the same. The program was a hit. Listeners loved it and the network realized it. Today, Sally Jesse Raphael is a two-time Emmy-Award-winning host of her own television talk show reaching eight million viewers daily throughout the United States, Canada and the United Kingdom.

• Four-time Academy-Award-winning actress Katharine Hepburn was fired from several of her early stage roles. She was criticized for talking too fast, was considered ornery and difficult to work with, and was evaluated as too bony, thin and mannish to be on stage. Accom- panied by her unwavering determination, she sought the assistance of a voice and drama coach who nurtured her through a variety of stage roles. Eventually, one of her performances drew great reviews and led to a movie contract.

Jack Canfield, Mark Victor Hansen,
Hanoch McCarty and Meladee McCarty

Let Me Die!

Open your eyes and look for some man, or some work for the sake of men, which needs a little time, a little friendship, a little sympathy, a little sociability, a little human toil. . . . It is needed in every nook and corner. Therefore search and see if there is not some place where you may invest your humanity

Albert Schweitzer

As he was crossing an overpass on the Auto Mall Parkway outside San Jose, California, Rajon Begin couldn't believe what he was seeing. A muscular young man, dressed only in gym shorts and tennis shoes, slipped around an eight-foot-high, chain-link safety fence that bordered the overpass and started inching his way onto the narrow outside ledge.

"That's foolish," Begin thought, frowning. "What in the world is he doing? Is he some kind of daredevil? One slip and he's a goner."

Begin glanced into his truck's rearview mirror in an effort to see what was happening. But the road dipped, and he lost sight of the man. A moment or so later, he turned onto a ramp leading to U.S. 680 and home.

It was a warm September afternoon in 1994, and Begin had promised his three-year-old daughter, Monet, that he'd take her to the park. From the looks of the thickening rush-hour traffic, he was going to be late. Checking back as he swung onto 680, he could see the man still on the overpass. Something about his posture—the slumped shoulders, the bowed head—brought Begin to a sickening realization.

"My God!" he said out loud. "He's going to jump!"

Begin knew exactly what the man must be going through. When he was a boy, his father was seldom around, forcing his mother to work long hours as a secretary to support him and his sister. When his mother remarried, Begin and his stepfather did not get along. Begin ran away at 15, living with whatever family would take him in. More than once he contemplated taking his own life. But even in the darkest times he thought of how his mother had struggled against great odds and survived. If she hadn't given up, how could he?

Now, at the age of 27, Begin had everything he'd ever dreamed of—a wonderful family, a good job as a sales executive with a commercial printing company and a comfortable home. "I've got to go back!" Begin suddenly thought. He realized that he had no choice. It was his responsibility to share what he knew—that life gets better if you give it a chance. He owed to others the sort of kindness he had been shown in those earlier difficult times.

Veering off the highway at the next exit, he bogged down almost at once in heavy traffic. "I can't get stuck here!" he said out loud, and drove up over the curb, down an empty sidewalk and through a shopping center parking lot. Within minutes he was back on the Auto Mall Parkway.

At the overpass he slammed on his brakes and parked his truck on the wide concrete divider. The guy was still there. "Hey!" Begin yelled as he ran across the highway, dodging traffic. "Don't do that. Let's go have a beer and talk it over."

For a moment the eyes of the would-be jumper and the rescuer met. Then the jumper turned his head, staring down at the train tracks 50 feet below.

"Hold on," Begin called. "'I'm coming out there."

"Stay away," the jumper warned. "Nobody cares what I do."

"I care," Begin said, encouraged that he'd gotten a response. "I almost killed myself racing my truck here to talk to you."

Adrenaline pumping, Begin climbed onto the narrow ledge and edged his way, step by step, toward the man. Begin realized that he was the smaller of the two. He estimated the other man to be about six feet tall, weighing more than 200 pounds. The guy was facing the wire-mesh fence, clinging to it with both hands. His back was to the tracks below, and he was staring at them over his shoulder. As Begin got near, he noticed the man was shaking violently.

"Can I get to him in time?" he thought, inching closer and closer. He had begun to formulate a plan. But if he made one tiny miscalculation or the big man lunged at him, Begin realized he, too, could plummet to his death.

Still he acted without a second's hesitation. Gripping the fence tightly with his left hand, he swung his right foot out and around the jumper, planting it firmly on the ledge on the other side of the bigger man. Then he grabbed hold of the chain mesh with his right hand. With his body now spread-eagled behind the jumper, Begin had him pinned to the fence. The man couldn't jump without taking Begin with him.

"Let me go, damn you," the jumper pleaded. "Let me go. I want to die."

"It's okay, man," Begin said. "It's okay. Everything is going to be just fine." And for a moment the bigger man seemed to relax back against Begin's chest.

"I've bought some time," Begin thought. "But if I don't get help soon, we'll both die."

Brian Gundy, 41, a manufacturing manager at an engineering firm, usually worked late. But feeling restless and unable to concentrate, he had left work early that afternoon.

Obeying a sudden urge, he swung onto the Auto Mall Parkway, a route he hadn't traveled for nearly two years. He was daydreaming when he reached the overpass and noticed someone clinging to the outside of the fence. No one else was stopping, but Gundy, a devout Christian and a member of his company's emergency-response team, knew he had to act.

His first impulse was to call the police, but he could find no phone nearby. Pulling off the road, he ran toward the fence. Sizing up the situation as he approached, Gundy felt a surge of admiration for the man who evidently was risking his own life to save the jumper. It was, he thought, a remarkably brave thing to do.

"What's your name?" Gundy asked the big man gently when he reached the fence. It was the only thing he could think to do at the moment, hoping to distract and calm the man. To his surprise he got an answer.

"Charles. Charles Crawford."

"Charles, I'm Brian. What's wrong? Can we talk about this?"

Crawford was crying and barely coherent as he moaned, "I want to jump!" He began to push away from the fence.

Realizing there was no way he could help the rescuer maintain his grip, Gundy prayed aloud: "Please God, keep them alive. Give Charles the will to live."

Meanwhile, Chris Eyre, a 47-year-old money manager who was battling his way westbound in the heavy traffic, had also caught sight of the men clinging to the overpass fencing. As a Mormon lay minister, he had often counseled distraught people. He called the police on his cellular phone, then pulled onto the shoulder and ran to the scene.

At six feet, five inches, Eyre was 10 inches taller than Gundy. With his height advantage, Eyre was able to reach up the fence and wrap his fingers around Crawford's. He knew he couldn't prevent the man from jumping. It was simply a gesture of caring, of trying to calm him until police arrived. A powerful struggle began to play itself out, with one man begging to die and three others pleading with him to live.

By now Begin had been clinging desperately to the fence for almost 30 minutes, his chest against Crawford's back. Pressing close enabled him to keep a tighter grip, but he also wanted Crawford to feel in touch with another human being.

"Do you have a family?" Gundy asked.

"Three half-sisters," Crawford answered, his voice barely audible. "My birthday was two days ago. They didn't call. Neither did my mother."

The three continued to probe gently, hoping to keep Crawford's mind off his problems. In short, choppy replies he told them his age and that he lived nearby with his grandparents. Not much, but at least he was talking.

The pressure on Begin's fingers grew intense. Crawford turned and looked over his shoulder at Begin. "Get out of my way," he demanded. "I don't want to hurt you. I just want to die."

Begin wondered how much longer he could hold on. Looking up, he noticed that four police cars and a fire truck had arrived on the scene. An officer approached slowly.

"Don't worry about my uniform," he said to Crawford. "We're all just men here. We want to help. Do you want to get off the ledge now?"

Crawford shook his head no.

Eyre had hoped that a police crisis negotiator would take over. But the police thought the three men had forged a bond, however tenuous, with Crawford and had a better chance than strangers to talk him down.

Noticing Crawford's powerful build, Eyre had a hunch. "Did you play football in high school?" he asked.

Crawford nodded. "Yeah, I was a linebacker at Irvington High."

Eyre thought quickly. Eric Widmar, a young man in his church, had also played football at the same school. He asked if Crawford knew him.

"Oh, yeah!" Crawford said, visibly brightening. "We played together."

"At last," Eyre thought. "Some common ground."

For what seemed a very long time, the men talked— about football, the San Francisco 49ers, fishing. Slowly Eyre began to realize that an inexplicable bond was growing among the four men. And soon the painful story that had compelled Charles Crawford to want to take his life came tumbling out.

It was eerily similar to Begin's. Difficulties with his step - father had driven Crawford from his mother's home at an early age. He struggled in school, got into frequent fights and ended up in a juvenile detention center. Still he seemed to be turning his life around—until that September day when his fiancee announced she was breaking off their relationship. It was then that he had heard a voice urging him to jump. "It's the best thing," the voice said. "Nobody wants you."

"Charles," Gundy said finally, "if you come over to this side of the fence, we're not going to forget you. A friend of mine has a boat. We can all go deep-sea fishing together."

"Just get out of my way and let me die!" Crawford cried. "Nobody cares."

"Look behind you!" Gundy responded. "There's a guy risking his life to save yours. Please don't do this."

Crawford turned and stared at Begin. Sobbing, he said, "Let me go!"

"No way," Begin answered, his face ashen but resolute. "If you go, I go! I'm not moving."

Crawford stared at Begin and then at the two others. He shut his eyes and stopped pushing. Finally he said softly, "I don't want to be out here anymore."

After the two exhausted men were pulled to safety, Crawford was whisked away by ambulance. Begin gave his story to the police, then drove slowly home, his mind spinning. He opened the front door with a shaking hand as Monet raced across the living room.

"Daddy!" she cried. "Where have you been? Are we going to the park?"

Kneeling, he hugged and kissed her. "We'll go tomorrow," he promised. "Today I had to help a friend."

In the days and weeks that followed the incident, all three men kept in touch with Charles Crawford. True to his word, Gundy arranged a deep-sea fishing trip for the four.

Crawford has become friends again with his former fiancee and is trying to deal with his painful past. He feels that he's been given a second chance to live. "I have gained strength from what these men taught me, that people do care about each other," he says. "One of them risked his life to save mine. I can never forget that."

Michael Bowker

It's Up to You

One song can spark a moment,
One flower can wake the dream.
One tree can start a forest,
One bird can herald spring.
One smile begins a friendship,
One handclasp lifts a soul.
One star can guide a ship at sea,
One word can frame the goal.
One vote can change a nation,
One sunbeam lights a room.
One candle wipes out darkness,
One laugh will conquer gloom.
One step must start each journey,
One word must start each prayer.
One hope will raise our spirits,
One touch can show you care.
One voice can speak with wisdom,
One heart can know what's true,
One life can make the difference,
You see, *it's up to you!*

Author Unknown

Unexpected

Service was as much a part of my upbringing as eating breakfast and going to school. It isn't something that you do in your spare time. It was clear that it was the very purpose of life. In that context, you're not obligated to win. You're obligated to keep trying, to keep doing the best you can every day.

Marian Wright Edelman

In the 1970s, I was the first female officer to work patrol duties at the Anchorage Police Department. I was sent to hundreds of domestic violence calls in my first years. One time, I was sent to a disturbance in Spenard, an area of town known for violence involving guns.

It was after midnight, the Saturday after Thanksgiving. The snow had stopped but the streets were slick with ice caused by the recent winds. There were only five officers and a sergeant on duty.

At the 11 P.M. fall-out, my sergeant jokingly told me "to get the lead out." I was known for staying longer than most officers at domestic violence calls. I had attended a

week's training on the San Jose Crisis Intervention
Method. Our chief decided that this method, which provides crisis counseling and referrals on the spot, was not
cost-effective for our department. But that did not stop
me from trying to provide referrals to fighting couples
who were ready to listen. The policing goal is to not go
back to the same place in the same shift.

I did not know what I would find as I approached the
darkened house. I listened and did not hear an argument in
progress. I did not hear anything from inside the residence.
My footsteps in the crunchy snow gave away my approach
to the house. I cautiously let myself into the residence and
saw a woman sitting on the kitchen floor. Next to her right
hand was a revolver. She was quietly crying. She was at the
dry crying, sighing stage. Her first words were, "What do
you want? Can't I die in peace?" I quickly picked up the
gun, unloaded it and looked for the light switch. There was
a chef's knife about two feet from her on the counter. I
searched her to be sure I had all the weapons. Leaving her
on the kitchen floor crying, I took the knife and gun with
me as I searched the rest of the house. We were alone.

I returned to the kitchen, and as I tried to help her up
from the floor, she started screaming: "You don't have the
right to stop me. I want to die!" She appeared to be seven
or eight months pregnant. I asked, "What about your
baby's life?"

She continued to cry, pouring out her problems. She
had no job, no income, the heat was due to be shut off
Monday, and her boyfriend had just beaten her again.
Her left eye was swollen, her maternity top was torn, and
she had defense wounds on her hands and arms. I went
to the refrigerator to get ice for her eye—there was no
food. I put the ice in a towel. She grabbed the towel from
me, putting it on her eye. She screamed at me again, "I
don't need any help!"

I talked to her about her baby. Where were her relatives? She told me about the boyfriend who had assaulted her. I asked if she wanted to press charges against him. Her answer was typical for the time. "He'll just get out of jail and beat me up again." She reluctantly gave me information on the suspect. She refused to go to a hospital or a doctor.

Fifteen minutes passed. Dispatch checked on me, asking how soon I could respond to the next call. Calls were backing up.

I asked her who I could call for her. I did not want to leave her alone knowing she could always find another weapon. I phoned a girlfriend of hers and a minister I knew from our ride-along program.

While we waited for them to arrive, I gave her pen and paper, telling her to write down the numbers as I gave them to her. By the time her friend arrived, she had a list of domestic violence counselors and the social service number to file for financial aid for the baby. We talked about people I knew who would hire a pregnant woman. She wrote down the names and phone numbers. The baby was not due until after Christmas so I suggested she could find a temporary job. She was most interested in working at the Anchorage Arts Council, making stage sets. At least, for the moment, she was thinking about the future and not about killing herself.

The minister arrived as her friend was making coffee. I asked them to get her to a hospital, taking the gun and knife for safekeeping. I left. Fifty minutes had passed since I first arrived.

At the end of the shift, the sergeant wanted to know what had taken me so long at the domestic violence in Spenard. The other officers listened, thinking I was going to be reprimanded again. I flippantly told him, "I saved the department hundreds of dollars in overtime. The homicide team did *not* need to be called out and we did *not* need to go back." He said dryly, "Okay, this time." Then he winked at me.

This domestic violence call was soon forgotten, overshadowed by the multitude of other calls, one day very much like the next, call after call.

Soon, it was time for Fur "Rondy." For 11 days each February, Anchorage changes into a busy tourist town. People from everywhere come to see the dog sled races, test their skills and drink hard. It is the Alaskan midwinter party for the public. For police officers, it means many long hours and overtime, want it or not. Many officers only see the Fur Rondy events as they perform their police duties.

At our house, my older kids liked to attend the Rondy Melodrama. One Sunday, we went to the evening performance.

During the intermission, my daughter, Sheila, and I went to the restroom. As we were standing in line, a lady came out of one of the cubicles, saw me and exclaimed, "Oh, Anne!" She came over and hugged me. This took me absolutely by surprise, because I didn't recognize her.

She told me her name and said she was running the lighting system for the Melodrama. Then I remembered her and asked if she once lived on Spenard Road. She smiled, shaking her head yes. We talked as if we were old friends. The baby was a girl. She had not seen the abuser since that night. She now had a regular job. She shared her plans for her future with me.

I introduced her to Sheila, who was 11. Sheila asked, "How do you know my mom?" She said, "Your mother saved my life." This comment caused everyone in the ladies' restroom to listen. She went on to say, "If she had not come along when she did, I would not be alive today." We talked until she had to return to her lighting board.

When we returned to our seats, Sheila told her brothers about the woman in the restroom. Just after the play started, Sheila turned to say something to me. She was alarmed to see tears running down my cheeks. "Mom, what's wrong?" I replied softly, "No one ever said 'thank you' before."

Detective Anne Newell

Scattered Memories

You have to have faith that there is a reason you go through certain things. I can't say I'm glad to go through pain, but in a way one must, in order to gain courage and really feel joy.

Carol Burnett

And now the tears come, two and a half decades later. I ache for all we lost in Vietnam—our buddies, our relatives, our innocence.

I'm no heroine. I joined the Army Nurse Corps to go to Europe; that's what my recruiter promised me. I was 21 years old when I was ordered to Vietnam. I stayed 364 days. I cared for the sick, the wounded and the dying. I did the best I could. I am only coming to know that now.

For almost 20 years, I never spoke about that time, that place—I buried my memories, my anger and a large part of "me" deep, so deep, just wanting to forget; wanting to feel peace.

I only spoke to Sue about it because she was there too. Years later in the Army Reserves, once again in fatigues and combat boots out on field exercises, we'd turn to each

other, never making the connection of physical circumstances. We'd tell each other funny war stories, and we'd
laugh. Then one of us would remember, and share, and
then we'd cry. It would be months or maybe a year before
we would repeat the scenario.

In 1982, the Vietnam Veterans Memorial (The Wall) was
placed in our nation's capital. I saw pictures of it and the
vets on television or in magazines, and it brought out
emotions in me that went way beyond tears. And I, like
many vets, knew it wasn't over. We knew we had to go
there. We didn't know why, we just knew we had to go.
The Wall was calling us home.

It took me five years to answer. Sue and I went
together. At first, we stayed far away in the trees. "Tree-
Vets," we're called. Then a picnic on the grass behind The
Wall where we could see the visitors' heads moving along
as their walk took them deep into the V of the black gran-
ite. Our first frontal maneuver came at night—arm-in-
arm, supporting each other, ready for retreat, we walked
the length of those names, our tears camouflaged by the
night. Even there, even then, we rarely spoke about the
war, not even to each other. And we never wore anything
or said anything that identified us as Vietnam veterans.

1992 was the 10th anniversary of the Vietnam Veterans
Memorial. Sue couldn't come, and I did two things I'd
never done before—I went alone and I went in uniform. I
wore my current dress uniform with the rank of
Lieutenant Colonel, and all the insignia, medals and dec-
orations that tell a very specific story to those who know
how to read it. I could never have anticipated what happened to me there. I wrote Sue that night:

> *I carried you with me when I went to The Wall. I had
> the strength to be there, but I didn't feel the entitlement.
> I did put on a brave front. No raggedy remnants of faded*

fatigues or sun-bleached boonie hats for me. I stood heads above the crowd—proud (at long last) in my Class A's. My chest of ribbons saying loud and clear, "I'm a vet, too. I was your nurse. Honor me. Reach out to me. Please, help me to heal."

And they came. They were there for you, Sue. Oh, I wish you could have been there! You would have been so touched; and it was you who deserved what I received. God, but it felt so good to cry the tears that for so long we held, and covered with our laughter, and let the years bury so deep. They came, the 40-something vets looking so much older than their years. Some with the same eyes that we saw back then, the pain still very much with them. They hugged me and held me, and most smiled through tears as they tried to speak. They want you to know they remember that you were there for them, and they're grateful. You saved some of them and cared for them and for their buddies. They love you. You were their nurse.

I saw him hesitate at the edge of the crowd, then urged on by a friend the WWI vet came forward. With crippled and deformed hands, he stood as tall as his 86 years allowed and saluted me. I smiled as my eyes filled with tears and returned his salute. He was mortified that he might cry. I hugged him as his friend took our picture. He spoke volumes in the simple words, "Thank you."

It was a strange déjà vu. Remember when the GIs would always take our pictures? They still do. And all those eyes looking at us—how we learned to look right in them and say, "It's okay, you're gonna be just fine."

It's not so hard to see The Wall now, to be near it, to feel its presence, to feel their absence. We're going to be okay. It's time to heal, my friend . . . to know that you did everything you could, and more; that it mattered that you touched those lives.

Next year we'll stand together when the Women's Memorial is dedicated, and we can begin to forgive ourselves for our imagined slights and shortcomings and our human frailties. And we can begin the process of healing ourselves and coming to peace with our memories. I love you, my friend.

Veterans Day 1993, the Vietnam Veterans Women's Memorial was dedicated in Washington, D.C. Thousands of women vets attended, and we were overwhelmed. We led the parade—the nurses, Red Cross workers, entertainers, women who worked in supply, administration, logistics and intelligence. The streets were lined with people applauding and crying. A vet sat high up on a tree branch yelling, "Thank you! Thank you!" A man in a flight suit stood at attention for over two hours, saluting as the women passed by. People handed us flowers and hugged us. One GI had a picture of his nurse taken July, 1964. He was trying to find her.

The women veterans find each other. We know, at last, that we are not alone, that we are not paranoid or crazy, but that we have a lot of work to do in order to heal. We talk to each other and find comfort as well as pain in our words and our tears. Now after so many years, the process has finally begun and we hold each other close and say, "Welcome home."

Lt. Col. Janis A. Nark

Snowed In

Never doubt that a small group of thoughtful, committed people can change the world, indeed it's the only thing that ever has.

Margaret Mead

If it takes a village to raise a child, then January 17, 1994, was the day it took a village to save a child.

Barbara Schmitt sipped coffee and watched the snow outside her window pile up. The city of Louisville, Kentucky, was paralyzed, with drifts up to two feet deep, but she and the two granddaughters she was helping to raise didn't mind. They were going to spend the day warm indoors, playing and watching the blizzard. Ashley, age six, chatted excitedly. Her three-year-old sister Michelle was subdued. Michelle was one of the hundreds of American children awaiting a new liver.

Waiting and praying were a daily routine for Barbara Schmitt, but today the prayers were more intense. Michelle had been showing danger signs that made an immediate liver transplant critical, but the telephone was as silent as the snowy scene outside.

Then at nine in the morning, the phone rang. Here was the news Barbara needed. A hospital in Omaha had located the right liver donor, they were sure it was a match for Michelle, and they needed her there within 12 hours.

Barbara couldn't tell what to do first—rejoice or despair. The greatest gift Michelle would ever receive was awaiting her, and here they were, snowbound, 600 miles away. "We're snowed in," Barbara told the medical coordinator on the line. "The airport is 17 miles away, trucks are jackknifing off the roads, and there's no way we're going to get there."

"Don't give up," the woman told Barbara. "You have 12 hours to reach Omaha, so start thinking!"

Fortunately, the phone lines were still working, so Barbara got to work. She started by calling Sharon Stevens, a hairdresser who runs Hair Angels, a fund for children with special needs. Sharon had already lined up a Lear jet and two pilots to fly the Schmitts to Omaha when transplant time came. How to get from the Schmitts' house to the jet was the big question, but Sharon was as determined as Barbara to make this work. "Start packing. I don't know how, but you're going to make it,"

Next, Sharon put out a call for help through the local radio station. WHAS broadcast continuous messages, inviting listeners to call in with ideas and suggestions. Teresa Amshoff heard the story and suggested that the church parking lot adjoining her house, only a mile from the Schmitts, would make a perfect helicopter landing pad. As precious minutes ticked away, the Amshoffs rushed from door to door, pleading for help to clear the lot. Neighbors, already exhausted from shoveling their own driveways, came without hesitation. Within half an hour, 50 volunteers were working in sub-zero winds to clear the area of snow.

Someone called Kim Phelps of Skycare, an airlift service, and he offered to dispatch a helicopter to take Michelle to the airport. The church lot was confirmed as a workable launch pad, and Kim got busy arranging rides to the church for the medical team.

In the meantime, Barbara called Lear jet pilot Jason Smith to be sure he could make it to the airport. Like everyone else, he and his co-pilot were snowbound, but he promised that they would be there. A policeman and neighbor were able to drive them to the jet just in time.

Finally, with dusk looming, WHAS sent a four-wheel vehicle to transport Michelle and her family to the church. When they pulled into the meticulously cleared parking lot, there were 150 people, leaning on shovels, surrounded by mountainous piles of snow. As fire trucks arrived to provide makeshift landing lights for the helicopter, the crowd mushroomed to 300, applauding and waving as the Schmitts flew off into the snowy night.

Michelle's transplant was a success. It was the success not only of a skilled medical team, a child with the fight to survive and a family that wouldn't give up—but the success of a whole village that found something much better to do on January 17 than to stay warm inside and watch the snow.

Susan G. Fey

Susie's Run

When you believe you can—you can!

Maxwell Maltz

In parenthood, we learn as much from our children as they do from us. They remind us of a time when we were full of ideas and hope, before we learned to doubt ourselves or see obstacles in our path.

Our daughter Susie was in the fifth grade when she faced her first lessons about life and death and compassion. Her classmate Jeff was diagnosed with leukemia. Besides missing a lot of school, Jeff grew weak and lost his hair. While some of the children reacted with rejection or ridicule, Susie chose caring, and she and Jeff became special friends.

During a period of remission, Susie and Jeff spent all their time together playing, studying and talking. They even participated in a couple of 5K races together, and the two became inseparable.

So it was a horrible blow to our daughter when the leukemia prevailed, the sickness returned, and her best friend slipped away. That's when our remarkable daughter showed us the best of her creativity and strength—and reminded us about the power of belief.

Susie wanted to do something that would help people remember Jeff. Since in health he had enjoyed running, she decided on a Jeff Castro Memorial Run, with the proceeds going to the Leukemia Society. When she came to us with her idea, we were proud and moved, but cautious. We knew that Susie had no concept of the magnitude of such a task, nor did she have the experience and knowledge to make it happen. We certainly didn't know how to organize a fund-raising run, so we listened and let the idea drop. Little did we know that Susie would keep trying until she found someone willing to help her.

Without telling us, Susie approached her teachers. They praised her for the idea, but they, too, explained why it wouldn't work. Besides all the time and effort involved, they told her, *she* would need the proper contacts and a tremendous amount of sponsorship money. They suggested a small jump-a-thon instead. Susie listened, said nothing, and moved along her way.

You can imagine our bewilderment when, a couple of weeks later, we started getting phone calls at home from Pepsi-Cola, Coors and other companies asking for Susie. They'd been contacted about sponsoring a run and needed more details. At this point, we knew our daughter had taken charge of her dream and we certainly weren't going to stand in the way. There *was* going to be a run— and we were going to take an active role in helping.

After months of planning, coordination and fund-raising, the Jeff Castro Run for Leukemia took place. And was it a success? You bet! Over $20,000 was raised, with half covering the expenses and a check of $10,000 proudly handed over to the Leukemia Society. All because a little girl who loved a little boy had a vision that no one could change.

Thomas R. Overton

The Right Thoughts Riding
in My Mind

Success is a state of mind.

Joyce Brothers

When I started riding a bike a couple of years ago, I didn't think my involvement would ever be more serious than the occasional short ride. But as I built strength, my friends encouraged me to step up my training and try some longer trips, The first one to come along was a 150-mile trek, the MS-150, an annual event that raises money to fight multiple sclerosis.

When I registered, the idea seemed terrific—support a worthy cause while going for the distance—and I trained with enthusiasm. But as the time for the ride approached, my self-doubts gained ground over my endurance. I still wanted to raise money for the charity, but I didn't really want to bike all those miles for two days straight.

The ride began on a beautiful Sunday morning in the tranquil Georgia countryside, and for the first few hours I felt wonderful. This was just the experience I had imagined, and my spirits were high. But by the end of the day, I felt tired and irritable.

If the body is connected to the mind, here was proof in action. Every excuse my brain pushed out seemed to travel right down to my legs. "I can't handle this," became a leg cramp, and "everyone else is a better rider" translated into shortness of breath. I was sure I'd have to quit.

As I topped the crest of a hill, the magnificent sunset kept me going for a few minutes more. Then in the distance, silhouetted against the bright red sun, I saw a lone rider pedaling very slowly. I noticed that the person looked different in some way, but I couldn't tell why. So I pushed myself to catch up. There she was, peddling along slowly but steadily, with a slight and determined smile on her face—and she had only one leg.

My focus changed in that instant. For a whole day I'd been doubting my body. But now I knew—it wasn't the body, but the *will* that would help me reach my goal.

It rained all the second day. I never saw the one-legged biker again, but I pushed on without complaining, knowing she was out there with me somewhere. And at the end of the day, still feeling strong, I completed the 150th mile.

Kathy Higgins

A Tale of Canine Courage

The ice looked like daggers hanging from the gutter outside my bedroom window that winter day in 1968 when I first laid eyes on Fritzy. We piled in the family wagon that morning and headed out past the frozen corn fields and icy streams to the county kennels. We were going to get a dog.

I pressed my nose against the car window, breathed on the cool glass, and wondered what he would be like. Would he shake hands, roll over and chase squirrels? Each passing fence post drew me nearer to my most cherished aspiration—a dog of my own.

The pandemonium as we walked through the kennel door was deafening. How we would wade through the canine chaos to make our decision was beyond me. Then, right in the middle of the tumult, silence caught my eye. He was sitting quietly and confidently in a corner cage, seemingly oblivious to the rancor raging around him.

When I approached, he lifted his paw between the bars, and I took it. A handwritten sign at the top of his stall read, "Collie/Shepherd." He pressed his nose against the door, and I rubbed his head. Ten minutes later he was sitting in the back seat of our car.

"His name is Fritzy," Grandmother announced that night as we watched him wolf down his inaugural meal. "After your father's first dog." And so it was.

Fritzy adjusted quickly to life at our little inn in the North Carolina mountains. Whenever guests would arrive, he would trot out to greet them. When they took their afternoon strolls, he was a cheerful escort. Fritzy's walking services became so popular that Dad had to finally institute a sign-up sheet to satisfy all the walkers vying for his camaraderie.

When we sold the inn and moved to town five years later, Fritzy settled into restful retirement. The highlight of his day was when I came bounding through the front door after school. He would slip and slide across the tile entryway and then leap into my arms as if he had just won the doggy lottery.

One Friday afternoon my father announced that we were going away for the night. Each year we took a journey across the mountains to his hometown of Knoxville, Kentucky, for a day of outlet shopping and sightseeing. As we loaded up the car, Dad informed me that the motel where we would be staying did not allow dogs, and therefore Fritzy wasn't coming with us.

"He'll be fine," he assured me "I left him extra food and it's only for the night. He won't even know we're gone."

My heart sank like a bowling ball in a swimming pool. We had never left Fritzy alone overnight. What would he do? What would he think?

As we pulled away down the street, Fritzy stood watching from the edge of the yard, his ears pricked up and his tail wagged skeptically, as if to say, "You must be kidding."

I couldn't sleep that night. All I could think about was a lonely, frightened dog wondering why we had deserted him. It was just after six o'clock when we rolled into our driveway the next evening. There was no enthusiastic greeting. No euphoric yelping. No Fritzy.

Night fell and no sign of him. We went from neighbor to neighbor, house to house. Each shake of the head drove me closer to despair.

"Please, God," I prayed kneeling by my bed that night. "Bring Fritzy home safe."

But a week passed and no Fritzy. I went to school and tried to concentrate, but all I could do was think about my missing dog somewhere out there wandering the lonely backroads.

Each afternoon I would bolt out of school and run all the way home. But when I burst through the door and into the house, I would be greeted only by stillness and my mother's sad smile.

"What's taking God so long?" I asked mother one night as she tucked me in.

"Just hold onto hope," she said quietly.

"I don't think I have anymore hope," I whispered.

"As long as you come running up those steps every afternoon and fling open that door, you have hope, " she replied as she switched off my light.

It was right then and there that I decided my hope needed a little dusting off. I determined that, no matter how discouraged I was feeling, I was going to open that door with hope.

Another week passed and hope seemed harder and harder to come by. But I kept at it, determined to make it my own.

Then one afternoon, I arrived home to find Dad's truck parked in the driveway, and I wondered why he was home from work so early. I paused just outside the driveway and gathered my hope before going inside. When I was sure that I was all hoped up, I opened the door and stepped inside.

The hallway was empty, but I could hear the soft murmur of my parents' voices behind the kitchen door. All of a sudden, Mother cracked the door just enough to peer out at me.

"Hi, honey," she said smiling. "I have a surprise for you."

With that she swung wide the door, and Fritzy bolted past her like a wild boar. He slipped on the slick tile and crashed into the wall, got up and slipped again until he finally regained his balance and vaulted into my arms. I tumbled backward as he coated my face with licks.

Around the dinner table that night, Dad related how our intrepid dog had found his way several miles across town to the office of a friendly veterinarian who had taken care of him once years before. For two weeks, Fritzy had been fed, brushed and bathed, while he patiently waited for us to find him.

The vet had been listening to the radio that morning when our lost-dog announcement caught his attention and he knew he had the culprit.

That night as Dad tucked me in he asked if I had been afraid I would never see Fritzy again.

"No," I said. "I knew that if I kept opening that door, one day he was going to be behind it."

Robert Tate Miller

Don't Quit

When things go wrong, as they sometimes will,
When the road you're trudging seems all up hill,
When the funds are low and the debts are high,
And you want to smile, but you have to sigh,
When care is pressing you down a bit,
Rest, if you must—but don't you quit.

Life is queer with its twists and turns,
As every one of us sometimes learns,
And many a failure turns about
When he might have won had he stuck it out;
Don't give up, though the pace seems slow—
You might succeed with another blow.

Often the goal is nearer than
It seems to a faint and faltering man,
Often the struggler has given up
When he might have captured the victor's cup.
And he learned too late, when the night slipped down,
How close he was to the golden crown.

Success is failure turned inside out—
The silver tint of the clouds of doubt—
And you never can tell how close you are,
It may be near when it seems afar;
So stick to the fight when you're hardest hit—
It's when things seem worst that you mustn't quit.

Author Unknown

Persistence Pays Off

Like many young women, Joan Molinsky dreamed of a career on stage, entertaining the masses. She had a knack for making people laugh, so she opted for a career in comedy.

However, her parents were skeptical, despite their daughter's success in a number of small-time revues and local talent contests. Eager to see her perform in a club setting, Dr. Molinsky had his comedian-wanna-be daughter booked at the family's beach club in New Rochelle, New York. The show was the club's last of the summer, and Joan's first dinner engagement.

Miss Molinsky started her act with a funny song, but the audience's attention span lasted only as long as it took the dessert carts to visit their tables. In a matter of no time, the 300 people in attendance had resumed any and all conversations they'd had prior to the pretty, 20-something's introduction on stage.

Heartbroken and ignored, Joan ground her way through each of her numbers to the best of her ability. Uttering a meek "thank you" at the conclusion of her final song. Joan burst into the nearby kitchen, teary-eyed with embarrassment. Her parents were also embarrassed, not for their daughter so much as themselves. Their daughter had flopped, reinforcing their belief that Joan had no future in entertainment.

Later that night, Dr. Molinsky told Joan that she would have to give up her dream of comedy and pursue a more realistic career choice. His daughter went ballistic.

"I don't care what you say! You don't know," Joan screamed at her father. "I do have talent. It's my life. It's my choice how I live it."

The fight eventually resulted in Joan moving out of her family's home and returning to New York City. Living out of a local YWCA, she took up temporary work, while pursuing her dreams with a variety of troupes and shows. Her dedication eventually led to a stint with the prestigious Second City performers and a job in California as a writer and on-air "bait girl" for *Candid Camera.*

Despite her growing role on the show, host Allen Funt never could remember her first name, calling her everything from Jeri to Jeannie to Jackie.

It was during her time with *Candid Camera* that Joan received a call from *The Tonight Show,* whom she had petitioned and pestered for over a year for a guest shot. They wanted her to appear with Johnny Carson. Calling in sick at *Candid Camera,* Joan prepared for the chance of a lifetime.

Once on stage, Joan and Carson hit it off immediately, engaging in verbal jousts too funny to be scripted. In the end, Carson wiped tears of laughter from his eyes and said aloud to his millions of viewers, "God, you're funny. You're going to be a star."

The next day, dozens of appearance offers flooded in from all over the country, putting Joan on comedy's A-list. She also resigned from *Candid Camera* that day, much to the chagrin of an angry Funt, who'd watched his "sick" employee on Carson the night before.

Chomping down on a carrot stick, he chewed thoughtfully and said, "I think you're making a big mistake, Jill." From that point on, no one would ever misidentify or underestimate Joan Rivers again.

Curtis McAllister
Submitted by Christine Belleris
and Randee Goldsmith

I'll Do Anything!

My share of the work of the world may be limited, but the fact that it is work makes it precious.

Helen Keller

Jack had cerebral palsy. He was quadriplegic and used the restricted motion he had in one hand to push the lever that propelled his electric wheelchair. Although he was not one of my students, he often listened to my lectures and participated in discussion groups. I had a difficult time understanding his speech and relied heavily on classmates to interpret for him. He shared his personal concerns and frustrations with me, deeply touching my heart. He was so courageous to be so vulnerable!

One day after class, Jack came up to me and said he wanted to work. At the time I was training severely disabled adults to work at on- and off-campus jobs at Fresno City College. I asked Jack, "Where?"

He said, "With you in the cafeteria." Stunned for a moment, I thought about the skills needed to perform the tasks of bussing tables, loading dishwashers, sweeping,

mopping, stocking, etc. How could a person who is quadriplegic possibly participate in this type of training program? I couldn't answer. My mind was blank.

"What do you want to do, Jack?" I asked, hoping he
might have something in mind.

His response was firm. "I'll do *anything!*" he said with a
smile. Oh, how I loved his spirit and determination and
admired his conviction! We made arrangements to meet in
the cafeteria at 10:00 A.M. the following day. I wondered if
he would be punctual. Could he even tell time? The next
morning I heard his wheelchair 15 minutes early for his
appointment. I silently prayed for guidance and insight.

At 10:00 A.M., we met. By 10:01, Jack was ready to go to
work. His enthusiasm made his speech even more difficult to understand. In my endeavors to find a way for Jack
to participate meaningfully in a vocational training program, I ran into one obstacle after another. His wheelchair
kept him from getting too close to tables. He was unable
to use his hands except to grasp. I tried some adaptations
without success. Seeing my frustration, a kind-hearted
custodian offered to help. Within a half hour, he had pro-
vided a solution. He had shortened the handle of a floor
mop so that it fit comfortably under Jack's arm and could
be manipulated with one hand. The mop was positioned
to reach the table tops. With the other hand, Jack propelled his chair, wiping the surface of the tables as he
moved around.

Jack was in heaven! He was so proud to be an active par-
ticipant and not just an observer! As I watched, I noticed
that he could push chairs out of the way using his wheelchair. A new job was created for Jack: pushing chairs away
from tables that were designated for wheelchair use and
lining them up against the wall out of the way. Jack performed his job with gusto and pride. His self-esteem
soared! At last, he felt capable and worthwhile!

One day Jack came to me in tears. When I asked what was wrong, he explained to me that people were not letting him do his job. At first I didn't understand what he meant. Then I observed him trying to move chairs. It took so much effort on his part that well-intentioned students thought that he was struggling to get chairs out of his way and they would move the chairs for him. He tried to explain, but no one took the time to listen. The problem was solved when I made these cards for Jack to carry on his tray:

Hi! My name is Jack.
I am working in the cafeteria.
My job is to wipe down tables
And move certain chairs to the wall.
If you would like to help me,
PLEASE give me a big smile
And tell me what a good job
I am doing.

Jack displayed and shared these cards proudly. Students began taking Jack and his job seriously. That semester, he experienced the self-worth that comes when one feels acknowledged and supported. His determination will always be an inspiration to me, as I search for and find new ways for my students and I to overcome life's obstacles and be all we can be with our God-given talents.

Dolly Trout

Henri Dunant

He who has a why to live for can bear almost any how.

Friedrich Nietzsche

Henri Dunant, at age 30, was a wealthy Swiss banker and financier. His life would probably have continued much as it had except for one fateful day, June 24, 1859, that changed everything.

Dunant had been sent by his government to talk to Napoleon III. He was to discuss a business deal between the Swiss and the French that would benefit both. But Napoleon was not in Paris; he was on the plain of Solferino about to do battle with the Austrians.

Henri Dunant tried to reach the scene before the battle began, but he was too late. His carriage came to a halt on top of a hill that overlooked the battlefield.

Suddenly trumpets blared, muskets cracked, cannons boomed. The two cavalries charged and the battle was on. Henri Dunant, as if in a box seat at the theater, sat transfixed. He could see the dust rising, hear the screams of the injured, the dying. Dunant sat as if in a trance at the horror below him.

But the real horror was later—when he entered the small town after the battle was over. Every house, every building was filled with the mangled, the injured, the dead. Driven by pity at the suffering he saw all around him, Dunant stayed in the town for three days doing everything he could to help.

He was never the same man again. War was barbarous. The world should abolish it.

This was not the way to settle differences between nations. And most of all, there ought to be a worldwide organization to help people in times of suffering and chaos.

Henri Dunant returned to Switzerland, but in the next few years he became a fanatic on the subject of peace and mercy. He began to travel all over Europe preaching his message. Eventually his business suffered in the effort and he was soon broke. But he persisted.

At the first Geneva Conference, he carried on a one-man assault against war. As a result, the Conference passed the first international law against war—a movement that was to give birth eventually to both the League of Nations and the U.N.

In 1901, Dunant was awarded the first Nobel Peace prize. And though he was penniless and living in a poorhouse, he gave the entire prize to the worldwide movement he had founded.

Henri Dunant died in 1910 almost totally forgotten by the world. But Dunant needed no monument to mark his grave. As a symbol of the organization he had fathered, he had taken the Swiss flag, a white cross on a red background and reversed it: a red cross on a white background. The organization that became his everlasting monument was the Red Cross.

Bits & Pieces

8

ECLECTIC WISDOM

The universe is one great kindergarten for man. Everything that exists has brought with it its own peculiar lesson. The mountain teaches stability and grandeur; the ocean immensity and change. Forests, lakes, and rivers, clouds and winds, stars and flowers, stupendous glaciers and crystal snowflakes—every form of animate or inanimate existence, leaves its impress upon the soul of man. Even the bee and ant have brought their little lessons of industry and economy.

Orison Swett Marden

The Trouble Tree

Nothing can bring you peace but yourself.

Ralph Waldo Emerson

The carpenter I hired to help me restore an old farm-house had just finished a rough first day on the job. A flat tire made him lose an hour of work, his electric saw quit and now his ancient pickup truck refused to start. While I drove him home, he sat in stony silence. On arriving, he invited me in to meet his family. As we walked toward the front door, he paused briefly at a small tree, touching the tips of the branches with both hands.

When opening the door, he underwent an amazing transformation. His tanned face was wreathed in smiles and he hugged his two small children and gave his wife a kiss. Afterward he walked me to the car. We passed the tree and my curiosity got the better of me. I asked him about what I had seen him do earlier.

"Oh, that's my trouble tree," he replied. "I know I can't help having troubles on the job, but one thing for sure, troubles don't belong in the house with my wife and the children. So I just hang them up on the tree every night when I come home. Then in the morning I pick them up again.

"Funny thing is," he smiled, "when I come out in the morning to pick 'em up, there ain't nearly as many as I remember hanging up the night before."

Author Unknown

A Handle on Love

The summer of '86, my wife and I were heading east when we came upon an 18-wheeler. The driver was signaling to get into my lane, so I eased down on the brake. As the truck pulled ahead we heard on our CB radio, "Thank you, four-wheeler." We engaged in CB chat and asked him if he knew of a good place to eat. He said to follow him.

We sat together at the restaurant and asked him about his handle (CB name). It was Frankie the Clown. He said that he spends a lot of time on the road and many lonely nights in hotel rooms. He carries a clown suit with him, and sometimes during a layover, he dresses up and visits with children at the nearest hospital. A towering man with gigantic, rough-hewn hands, it was hard to imagine him in costume. Then he told us a story about why he did this. The twinkle in his soft brown eyes spoke volumes about his rewards.

> *I was pulling a load, nervous 'cause I was behind schedule. Just then, my engine starts to overheat so I took her to a garage. They told me to leave her while they waited for parts. So I checked into a hotel, bent out of shape because this was going to cost me big.*

Even though I felt like sulking alone in my room, I convinced myself to put on my clown outfit and head to the nearest hospital.

When I arrived, I told the nurse in charge of the children's ward why I was there. Reluctantly, she let me do my thing. I knocked softly on the first door but got no response. I carefully opened the door and saw a little boy, about three or four years old, lying in his bed and staring at the ceiling. I bounced over to him and said, "Hi! I'm Frankie the Clown. What's your name?" He continued to ignore me, his small lips pursed together. Fighting the urge to move on to the next room, I started my routine. Finally, I got a smile, which kept me going. Within minutes, the boy was laughing out loud and so was I. We were having so much fun that I hardly noticed the nurse as she came in, wrinkled her brow, then left. We began to talk. He told me his name was Johnny and he was four years old.

Just then, I noticed the room filling up with nurses, doctors and orderlies. Oops, what did I do? *I thought. Turning to the nurse, I apologized for making such a racket.*

She looked me straight in the eye and said, "Frankie, you've got it all wrong. You aren't a nuisance—you're a blessing! This little boy has been with us for three weeks and no one, I mean, no one has been able to get any response from him. We apologize for interrupting, but when I told my co-workers that the little boy in room 109 was talking and laughing, they had to see it for themselves!"

As I rode back to my hotel, I wasn't frustrated or mad because I was losing money. I was on top of the world. My load would be late and I still wouldn't be rich. But I had made a little boy in room 109 laugh, and I felt like a million bucks.

Paul Glanville

The Old Fisherman

The worst prison would be a closed heart.

Pope John Paul II

Our house was directly across the street from the entrance to the clinic of the Johns Hopkins Hospital in Baltimore. We lived downstairs and rented the upstairs rooms to outpatients at the clinic.

One summer evening, as I fixed supper, there was a knock at the door. I opened it to see a truly awful-looking old man. "Why, he's hardly taller than my eight-year-old," I thought as I stared at the stooped, shriveled body. Most appalling, his face was lopsided from swelling, red and raw. Yet his voice was pleasant as he said, "Good evening. I've come to see if you've a room for just one night. I came for a treatment this morning from the eastern shore, and there's no bus until morning." He told me he'd been hunting for a room since noon but with no success. "I guess it's my face. I know it looks terrible, but my doctor says with a few more treatments . . ."

For a moment I hesitated but his next words convinced

me, "I could sleep in this rocking chair on the porch. My bus leaves early in the morning." I told him we would find him a bed, but meanwhile he could rest on the porch.

I went inside and finished getting supper. When we were ready, I asked the old man if he would join us. "No, thank you. I have plenty." He held up a brown-paper bag.

When I had finished the dishes, I went out on the porch to talk with him for a few minutes. It didn't take long to see that this old man had an oversized heart crowded into that tiny body. He told me that he fished for a living to support his daughter, her five children and her husband, who was hopelessly crippled from a back injury. He didn't tell it by way of complaint. Every other sentence was prefaced with thanks to God for a blessing. He was grateful that no pain accompanied his disease, which was apparently a form of skin cancer. He thanked God for giving him the strength to keep going.

At bedtime, we put a camp cot in the children's room for him. When I got up in the morning, the bed linens were neatly folded and the little old man was out on the porch. He refused breakfast, but just before he left for his bus, haltingly, as if asking a great favor, he said, "Could I please come back and stay the next time I have to have a treatment? I won't put you out a bit, I can sleep fine in a chair." He paused a moment and then added, "Your children made me feel at home. Grownups are bothered by my face, but children don't seem to mind." I told him he was welcome to come again.

On his next trip, he arrived a little after seven in the morning. As a gift, he brought us a big fish and a quart of the largest oysters I had ever seen. He said he had shucked them that morning before he left so they would be nice and fresh. I knew his bus left at 4:00 A.M. and wondered what time he had to get up in order to do this.

Over the years he came to stay overnight with us, there was never a time that he did not bring us fish or oysters or vegetables from his garden. Other times we received packages in the mail, always by special delivery, fish and oysters packed in a box of fresh young spinach or kale, every leaf carefully washed. Knowing that he must walk three miles to mail these and how little money he had made these gifts doubly precious. When I received these little remembrances, I often thought of a comment our next-door neighbor had made after the fisherman left that first morning. "Did you keep that awful-looking old man last night? I turned him away. You can lose roomers by putting up such people." And maybe we did, once or twice. But oh, if only they could have known him, perhaps their illnesses would have been easier to bear. I know our family always will be grateful to have known him. From him we learned what it was to accept the bad without complaint and the good with gratitude to God.

Recently I was visiting a friend who has a greenhouse. As she showed me her flowers, we came to the most beautiful one of all, a golden chrysanthemum, bursting with bloom. But to great surprise, it was growing in an old dented, rusty bucket. I thought to myself, if this were my plant I'd put it in the loveliest container I had. My friend changed my mind. "I ran short of pots," she explained, "and knowing how beautiful this one would be, I thought it wouldn't mind starting in this old pail. It's just for a little while till I can put it out in the garden." She must have wondered why I laughed so delightedly, but I was imagining just such a scene in heaven. "Here's an especially beautiful one. He won't mind starting in this small, ugly body." But that's behind us now. Long ago in God's garden, how tall this lovely soul must stand!

Mary Bartels

I Was Dying

First I was dying to finish high school and start college.
And then I was dying to finish college and start working.
And then I was dying to marry and have children.
And then I was dying for my children to grow old enough
   for school so I could return to work.
And then I was dying to retire.
And now, I am dying . . . and suddenly I realize I forgot to
   live.

Anonymous
Submitted by Nicole Zablocki

Encouragement

Dante Gabriel Rossetti, the famous 19th-century poet and artist, was once approached by an elderly man. The old fellow had some sketches and drawings that he wanted Rossetti to look at and tell him if they were any good, or if they at least showed potential talent.

Rossetti looked them over carefully. After the first few, he knew that they were worthless, showing not the least sign of artistic talent. But Rossetti was a kind man, and he told the elderly man as gently as possible that the pictures were without much value and showed little talent. He was sorry, but he could not lie to the man.

The visitor was disappointed, but seemed to expect Rossetti's judgment. He then apologized for taking up Rossetti's time, but would he just look at a few more drawings—these done by a young art student?

Rossetti looked over the second batch of sketches and immediately became enthusiastic over the talent they revealed. "These," he said, "oh, these are good. This young student has great talent. He should be given every help and encouragement in his career as an artist. He has a great future if he will work hard and stick to it."

Rossetti could see that the old fellow was deeply moved. "Who is this fine young artist?" he asked. "Your son?"

"No," said the old man sadly. "It is me—40 years ago. If only I had heard your praise then! For you see, I got discouraged and gave up—too soon."

Anonymous
From Brian Cavanaugh's The Sower's Seeds

Guess You Just Had to Have
Known Gladys

I'm not a has-been. I'm a will be.

Lauren Bacall

On her 95th birthday, my fiancé introduced me to his grandmother, Gladys Attwood. Her eyes twinkled, as I pulled up a chair to sit beside her, just as one of her three daughters prepared a video for us all to enjoy. Helen explained that the video was a compilation of the three television commercials that Gladys starred in the year before for a local car wash. Larry Dahl, owner of the Wash n' Well Car Wash had telephoned the minimal care facility where Gladys resided to see if there was a "spunky old lady" there with the charisma to pull off what he had in mind. Marge Siegfried, co-manager at the Royal Oaks Retirement Home, didn't think twice. They had "just the right person!"

"Just give me the works, Sonny!" she'd say as she pulled up to the attendant. Out of the car, she'd race around with her cane (the film was accelerated), kicking the tires, and tapping the attendants, as they scrubbed and buffed and shined. At the end she'd exclaim, "Well, I sure gave those boys the works!" and she'd smile and wink, the wink that won her recognition all over the town of Medford, Oregon. How she laughed when the video was over!

Once the crowd of family members around us thinned, and the flood of compliments slowed, I found myself listening intently to Gladys. A breast cancer survivor, she was active in the American Cancer Society's local cancer support group. "You know the young people that have had cancer, if they can see that you can have it and live to be 95, it does something for them," she said.

Our conversation continued and soon she shared her thoughts on the latest happenings in politics and world affairs. I was taken aback with the acute sharpness of this former champion college basketball player and teacher's mind whose knowledge and complex thought processes of current affairs put me to shame. It wasn't long before I was left far behind in awe.

Partly in an effort to save myself and partly because I was so amazed, I asked, "Tell me, Grandma, how ever did you manage to grow so old yet stay so young?"

Gladys leaned her warm, wrinkled face in closer to mine, her gray eyes shining behind her metal-framed glasses. "I'll tell you, Diane. A long time ago, a nurse told me that if you laugh a lot, you live longer, so . . . I laugh a lot . . . and my four boyfriends keep me going!"

"Your four boyfriends?!?!" I exclaimed.

"Haven't I told you? Well . . . every morning I get up with Will Power. Then I go for a walk with Arthur Itis. I come home with Charlie Horse. Then I go to bed with my favorite . . . Ben Gay."

Diane Brucato Thomas

Inspiration

He stares out the window
     at the children below
     who were playing so freely,
     laughing.
He sits in the dim room on the second floor
confined, but in his mind.
Each day, he's there.
Rarely does he move from his chair
     It's just too much effort
     to use the cane.

The laughter—what sweetness to his ears.
Was he ever young like that?
Did he play in the street?
Was he ever free of worry?
They are—so obviously.

A little boy notices him one day
     just watching them play.
The boy gives him a toothless grin,
     and he does the same—

It is so strange for his face
to crease in that long forgotten way.

His friend pays him a visit—
   riddled with scolds and advice.
"You're just waiting, aren't you? Waiting to die."
He makes no motion and does not turn from the window
   transfixed on the children below.
His friend leaves.
   He doesn't notice when,
   and he doesn't recall what was said
   save only one thought—
      Was he?
      Was he waiting to die?
He never thinks with any level of depth.
He never thinks about much
since the time
the time he keeps out of his mind
the time his wife died.

They push, they play
their laughter is fresh.
He lifts from his chair and leans
   against the window beam.
   He stands, watching the children.
The toothless boy looks up searchingly.
   The boy sees him
   and waves with excitement.
      He waves back.

He walks now with his cane
   around the small room.
What inspired him to do so?
He does not know.

"Hi," says a voice behind him.
With effort he turns around.
The toothless boy is smiling,
    his little arms swinging.
Perspiration collects on his forehead.
He slowly wipes his face with his free hand,
    leaning heavily on his cane.

"How are you, sir?"
He nods.
"Would you like to come outside and play?"
"Play?" he says softly.
"Yes! It's stickball today."
"No, no. I can't play."
"Why, sir?" The boy is confused.
"I'm too old to play."
"It's okay if you're slower than us. We all agreed.
    It's funner to play than watch all the time—don't you
        think?"
"I—I suppose."

The boy quickly goes to his side
    and leads him to the door.
He goes.
The boy helps him down the stairs
    and opens the door to the outside—
His face feels the winter cold
His eyes feel the morning light.
He trembles a little, and the boy
    holds his hand firmly.
His cane slips from his grasp,
    the boy steadies it securely.
He coughs twice, his body begins to shake.
The boy looks up at him in concern, "Are you all right?"

He nods and meets the boy's eyes
   the eyes of youth, sparkling and alive.

"Hey, everyone! This is uh, sir, what is your name?"
"Donald."
"This is Donald, and he's going to play!"

Lea Gambina

State of Mind

If you think you are beaten, you are;
if you think you dare not, you don't.
If you like to win, but think you can't,
it's almost a cinch you won't.

If you think you'll lose, you're lost;
for out in the world we find
success begins with a fellow's will;
it's all in the state of mind.

If you think you're outclassed, you are;
you've got to think high to rise,
you've got to be sure of yourself
before you can win the prize.

Life's battles don't always go
to the stronger or faster man;
but sooner or later the man who wins
is the man who thinks he can.

Author Unknown
Submitted by Wrae Duncan

101 Gifts to Give All Year Long

1. Smile.
2. Provide a shoulder to lean on.
3. Pat someone on the back.
4. Say "thank you."
5. Give an unexpected kiss . . .
6. . . . or a warm hug.
7. Say, "You look wonderful!" and mean it.
8. Rub a tired back.
9. Whistle when you're feeling down.
10. Send a thank-you card to an old teacher.
11. Say "Good morning," even if it isn't.
12. Mail an unexpected and caring letter to an old friend.
13. Place a surprise phone call.
14. Wash the dishes when it's not your turn.
15. Empty the trash when it's not your turn.
16. Ignore a rude remark.
17. Send a "one-minute love call."
18. Start off someone's day with a joke or funny story.
19. Make coffee at the office for your secretary, for example.
20. Save the want ads for a job hunter.
21. Write an encouraging letter to the editor.

22. Take Grandma or Grandpa to lunch.
23. Send a "thinking of you" card.
24. Wave and smile at a parking enforcement officer.
25. Pay your bills on time.
26. Give your used clothes to a needy person.
27. Pass on some good news. Don't pass on the gossip.
28. Say something nice to someone.
29. Lend a favorite book. Don't nag to get it back.
30. Return a friend's favorite book.
31. Play catch with a little kid.
32. Help someone figure out a solution instead of giving advice.
33. Take a box of homemade cookies to work.
34. Visit an elderly shut-in.
35. Laugh at a boring joke.
36. Tell your partner that she is beautiful.
37. Serve breakfast in bed and clean up afterward.
38. Clean the house for Mom and Dad.
39. Share a dream.
40. Walk with your partner on a regular basis.
41. Keep a confidence.
42. Try to understand a teenager. Try again and again. Succeed.
43. Let someone ahead of you in line.
44. Catch someone "doing it right" and say, "Great job!"
45. Say please.
46. Say yes when you'd rather say no.
47. Explain patiently.
48. Tell the truth, but with kindness and tact. Ask, "Does the other person really need to hear this?"
49. Encourage a sad person.
50. Spread a little joy.
51. Do a kind deed anonymously.
52. Share your umbrella.
53. Leave a funny card under a windshield wiper.

54. Tape a love note to the refrigerator.
55. Give someone a flower from your garden.
56. Share a beautiful sunset with someone you love.
57. Say, "I love you" first. Say it often.
58. Share a funny story with someone whose spirits are dragging.
59. Free yourself of envy and malice.
60. Encourage some youth to do her best.
61. Share an experience and offer hopeful-ness.
62. Find the time. Yes, you can. It involves making new choices.
63. Think things through.
64. Listen.
65. Examine your demands on others. Give some of them up.
66. Lighten up. Find the funny side of a situation.
67. Take a quiet walk when you feel like blowing your top.
68. Be a friend.
69. Be optimistic.
70. Express your gratitude.
71. Read something uplifting to someone.
72. Do what you value and value what you do.
73. If you see litter on the sidewalk, pick it up instead of walking over it.
74. Be genuine.
75. Walk tall.
76. Never miss an opportunity to be affectionate to your loved ones.
77. Invite a loved one to snuggle and lie on the grass on a sum-mer's night while you look at the stars.
78. Look for something beautiful in one person everyday.
79. Take someone on a surprise outing.
80. Ask a friend for help, even when you don't need it.
81. Be quiet in a library.
82. Help someone change a tire.

83. Tell a bedtime story to a little one or ask the little one to tell you a story.
84. Share your vitamin C.
85. Give a blanket to a homeless person
86. Mail someone a poem.
87. Leave your letter-carrier a little gift.
88. Point out the beauty and wonder of nature to those you love.
89. Allow someone a mistake.
90. Allow yourself several mistakes.
91. Take someone to the circus.
92. Use just one parking space.
93. Consider a different point of view.
94. Let your partner win at golf.
95. Forgive an old grudge.
96. Talk with a lonely child.
97. Laugh at an old joke.
98. Take the kids to the park.
99. Be the "eyes and ears" for your friends.
100. Buy the wine your partner likes.
101. Let go of the urge to be critical of someone.

Hanoch and Meladee McCarty
Excerpted from Acts of Kindness

Who Is Jack Canfield?

Jack Canfield is one of America's leading experts in the development of human potential and personal effectiveness. He is both a dynamic, entertaining speaker and a highly sought-after trainer. Jack has a wonderful ability to inform and inspire audiences toward increased levels of self-esteem and peak performance.

He is the author and narrator of several bestselling audio- and videocassette programs, including *Self-Esteem and Peak Performance, How to Build High Self-Esteem, Self-Esteem in the Classroom* and *Chicken Soup for the Soul—Live.* He is regularly seen on television shows such as *Good Morning America, 20/20* and *NBC Nightly News.* Jack has coauthored numerous books, including the *Chicken Soup for the Soul* series, *Dare to Win* and *The Aladdin Factor* (all with Mark Victor Hansen), *100 Ways to Build Self-Concept in the Classroom* (with Harold C. Wells) and *Heart at Work* (with Jacqueline Miller).

Jack is a regularly featured speaker for professional associations, school districts, government agencies, churches, hospitals, sales organizations and corporations. His clients have included the American Dental Association, the American Management Association, AT&T, Campbell Soup, Clairol, Domino's Pizza, GE, ITT, Hartford Insurance, Johnson & Johnson, the Million Dollar Roundtable, NCR, New England Telephone, Re/Max, Scott Paper, TRW and Virgin Records. Jack is also on the faculty of Income Builders International, a school for entrepreneurs.

Jack conducts an annual eight-day Training of Trainers program in the areas of self-esteem and peak performance. It attracts educators, counselors, parenting trainers, corporate trainers, professional speakers, ministers and others interested in developing their speaking and seminar-leading skills.

For further information about Jack's books, tapes and training programs, or to schedule him for a presentation, please contact:

The Canfield Training Group
P.O. Box 30880 • Santa Barbara, CA 93130
phone: 805-563-2935 • fax: 805-563-2945
To e-mail or visit our Web site:
http://www.chickensoup.com

Who Is Mark Victor Hansen?

Mark Victor Hansen is a professional speaker who, in the last 20 years, has made over 4,000 presentations to more than 2 million people in 32 countries. His presentations cover sales excellence and strategies; personal empowerment and development; and how to triple your income and double your time off.

Mark has spent a lifetime dedicated to his mission of making a profound and positive difference in people's lives. Throughout his career, he has inspired hundreds of thousands of people to create a more powerful and purposeful future for themselves while stimulating the sale of billions of dollars worth of goods and services.

Mark is a prolific writer and has authored *Future Diary*, *How to Achieve Total Prosperity* and *The Miracle of Tithing*. He is coauthor of the *Chicken Soup for the Soul* series, *Dare to Win* and *The Aladdin Factor* (all with Jack Canfield) and *The Master Motivator* (with Joe Batten).

Mark has also produced a complete library of personal empowerment audio- and videocassette programs that have enabled his listeners to recognize and use their innate abilities in their business and personal lives. His message has made him a popular television and radio personality, with appearances on ABC, NBC, CBS, HBO, PBS and CNN. He has also appeared on the cover of numerous magazines, including *Success*, *Entrepreneur* and *Changes*.

Mark is a big man with a heart and spirit to match—an inspiration to all who seek to better themselves.

You can contact Mark at:

P.O. Box 7665
Newport Beach, CA 92658
phone: 714-759-9304 or 800-433-2314
fax: 714-722-6912
Web site: http://www.chickensoup.com

Who Is Hanoch McCarty?

Hanoch McCarty is one of America's most sought-after keynote speakers. He is famous for his high energy, the appropriateness of his examples and stories, the drama and humor of his presentations, and the fact that he always interacts with his audiences in the most exciting way. He researches and custom designs each presentation.

Hanoch gives over 100 presentations each year all over the world. He has spoken in 16 countries including mainland China, Japan and Norway. He has spoken in most major cities in the United States as well. His client list includes: Quad/Graphics Corporation, Johnson & Johnson, Ortho Biotech, the U.S. Department of Agriculture, the U.S. Department of the Interior, the Internal Revenue Service, the U.S. Forest Service, Houston Public Schools, Dade County Schools, Broward County Schools, Nebraska Association of School Administrators, the University of Phoenix and similar groups all over the country. He speaks to school systems, college faculties, professional associations, medical practices, health maintenance organizations, dental groups, hospital staffs, law practices and industry groups.

He is the author of 16 books and training programs, including: *Self-Esteem in the Classroom: The Experts Speak; Growing Pains in the Classroom; Ten Keys to Successful Parent Involvement; Weekends: Great Ideas for Memorable Adventures;* and *Speaking to the Heart.* With his wife Meladee, he is coauthor of three books, including the bestseller, *Acts of Kindness: How to Create a Kindness Revolution; A Year of Kindness: 365 Ways to Spread Sunshine;* and *The Daily Journal of Kindness.*

Hanoch's presentations have included *The Hidden Power of Kindness in the Workplace; Self-Esteem: The Bottom Line in Employee Motivation and Productivity;* and many presentations for public and private schools on the connection between self-esteem and school achievement.

Hanoch also conducts programs for teens including *Kindness Is a Chain Reaction* and *The Ten Secrets of Life Success.* To contact him, write or call:

Hanoch McCarty & Associates
P.O. Box 66
Galt, CA 95632-0066
phone: 209-745-2212 • fax: 209-745-2252
e-mail: kindness@softcom.net

Who Is Meladee McCarty?

Meladee McCarty is a professional educator and dynamic speaker in the field of special education and inclusionary education. She is a Program Specialist for the Sacramento County Office of Education. She works to provide inclusional education settings for children with disabilities and presents a variety of trainings to educators on *Kindness in the Workplace; Communication and Team Building; Self-Esteem in the Classroom; Humor in the Learning Process* and *Focusing on the Disruptive Child.* She has extensive experience helping schools and other institutions meet the needs of disabled students and workers.

Meladee is the coauthor, with her husband Hanoch McCarty, of *Acts of Kindness: How to Create a Kindness Revolution; A Year of Kindness: 365 Ways to Spread Sunshine* and *The Daily Journal of Kindness.* They have traveled all over the United States and Norway together working with educators and business professionals on the goal of bringing more kindness and altruism into the world, workplace, home, community and classroom. Meladee and Hanoch have a wonderful time working and playing together. Meladee is a master at using appropriate humor to defuse tension and conflict.

Meladee and her husband Hanoch are the proud parents to Macallister Dodds, Stephanie Dodds, Ethan Rand McCarty and Shayna Liora Hinds. Of all the many opportunities she has had in her life, being the mother and wife of such a loving family is her most cherished role.

It is Meladee's goal to bring more kindness into the world and create a positive impact on those with whom she comes in contact. She is deeply touched and encouraged by the contributors to this book and the many wonderful kind and loving acts of altruism they have shared that keeps recreating a world that is a better place for all of us.

To contact Meladee for more information about her programs:

The Kindness Revolution
P.O. Box 66
Galt, CA 95632-0066
phone: 209-745-2212 • fax: 209-745-2252
To order autographed copies of Meladee's books,
call 800-KINDNESS

Contributors

Joyce Andresen is a medical social worker at Marengo Memorial Hospital. She lives in Keystone, Iowa with her husband, Ron and her two daughters.

Bits & Pieces, the magazine that inspires the world, has motivated and amused millions for almost 30 years. For your free issue, call 1-800-526-2554. Available in English, Spanish and Japanese.

Sister Carleen Brennan is a School Sister of Notre Dame. She is a teacher, author and lecturer and has been involved in education and administration for 45 years. In her retirement, she has shared her rich background experience with teachers and parents. She can be reached at 1402 Prior Ave. S., St. Paul, MN 55116.

Jennings Michael Burch is an internationally recognized author and speaker. His autobiography, *They Cage the Animals at Night,* chronicles his childhood experiences through orphanages and foster homes. He speaks to children and adults about family, values, kindness and honor. He strives to eliminate the ridicule of children by other children and succeeds. He can be reached at 2 Elm St., Chappaqua, NY 10514 or call 914-238-3031.

Fr. Brian Cavanaugh, TOR has compiled more than 40 handwritten journals of quotations, anecdotes and stories. Drawing upon this collection, he writes *Apple Seeds,* a monthly quote letter of motivation and inspiration. These journals have also resulted in four books published by Paulist Press: *The Sower's Seeds: 100 Inspiring Stories for Preachers, Teachers and Public Speakers; More Sower's Seeds: Second Planting; Fresh Packet of Sower's Seeds: Third Planting* and *Sower's Seeds Aplenty: Stories of Wit, Whimsy and Wisdom.* Fr. Brian can be contacted at Franciscan University, Steubenville, OH 43952, or call 614-283-6441.

Diana L. Chapman has been a newspaper journalist for more than 11 years, having worked at such newspapers as the *LA Times, The San Diego Union* and *LA Copley Newspapers.* She specializes in touching human interest stories and is currently working on a book on health issues, since she was diagnosed with multiple sclerosis in 1993. She has been married for seven years and has one son, Herbert "Ryan" Hart. She can be reached at 837 Elberon #3A, San Pedro, CA 90731 or call 310-548-1192.

Cheryl L. Costello-Forshey is a writer whose specialty is poetry. She writes memorials and also offers a unique gift idea called *Photographic Verse©.* All work is original and customer personalized. For information about either, send a SASE to 36240 S. 16th Rd., Barnesville, OH 43713.

Al Covino became an outstanding teacher, coach of various sports and later in his career became a school principal. He was an astute observer of people and recognized the compassion and kindness they displayed in their reactions to situations as they occurred. Al was a true friend, a great teacher, a great coach and advisor. He believed in helping people.

Donald Curtis has authored thirty bestselling books. Dr. Curtis founded and built the Unity Church of Dallas, one of the largest metaphysical congregations in the world, where he was minister for twenty-three years. He left that position in 1993 to devote full time to writing, lecturing and teaching. He has appeared widely on television and radio for many years including *Oprah!* Dr. Curtis may be reached at P.O. Box 258, Desert Hot Springs, CA 92240 or call 800-428-2794.

Doris W. Davis is a writer who aims to deliver screenplays that glorify God and transform lives (including her own) through the healing power of drama. Bozeman, Montana, is her home although she currently resides in Los Angeles near her four children. She can be reached at 213-730-1329 or call 406-585-9290.

Pamela J. deRoy resides in southern Wisconsin. After raising her children, Scott and Lisa, and after being caregiver to her late husband, Bill, who was totally disabled for 11 years, she has returned to her first love—writing! Juggling her job, volunteer work and writing, she has recently completed a book for pre-teen girls and is working on several short stories.

Dauna Easley is a teacher, speaker and freelance writer. She has a special interest in motivation and self-esteem issues. She is a frequent speaker at teacher conventions, parent organizations and women's groups. She is the parent of two daughters. Her youngest daughter was born with cerebral palsy and contracted brain cancer when she was five. Her story in this book describes the important lessons her daughter has taught her. She can be reached at 7929 Thistlewood Ct., West Chester, OH 45069 or call 513-777-9056 or 800-858-3324.

Andy Entwistle grew up in Needham, Massachusetts where his story takes place. He graduated from Northeastern University and is a major in the U.S. Army. Married with two children, Andy writes as a hobby and has published over a dozen articles and short stories.

Susan G. Fey writes for *The Corydon (Indiana) Democrat* and has contributed to a number of national newspapers and magazines including *Glamour, Ladies' Home Journal, The (Nashville) Tennessean* and *The (Indianapolis) Star.* She may be reached at P.O. Box 126, Corydon, IN 47112.

Clifford and Jerie Furness love the Lord, love each other and love every pastorate to which they have been appointed. Clifford has been a United Methodist minister since 1959 and Jerie is his secretary.

Janice M. Gibson is a teacher and freelance writer. Publishing credits include a children's poem and several articles for parents of preschoolers. Her biggest project was a joint effort with her husband Greg, writing lyrics to his children's dinosaur songs. To purchase a tape, write to Dat's Music, 14906 E. Stanford Dr., Aurora, CO 80015 or call 303-699-4576.

Paul Glanville lives in Shreveport, Louisiana, and is excited about seeing his first story published. In his spare time, he enjoys studying history, spending time with his six children and 15 grandchildren and working with the youth group at his church.

Bob Greene is a syndicated columnist with national bestsellers including *Hang Time: Be True to Your School,* and with his sister, D. G. Fulford, *To Our Children's Children: Preserving Family Histories for Generations to Come.* His new book is *The 50-Year Dash: The Feelings, Foibles and Fears of Being Half-a-Century Old.*

Kathy Higgins is employed by a multinational company in the leisure entertainment industry. She is an active member of Atlanta Unity Speakers, a member club in Toastmasters International. She enjoys writing, speaking and sports, including biking, running, racquetball and hiking.

Linda DeMers Hummel is a freelance writer and college english instructor. She can be reached at 2423 Hartfell Rd., Timonium, MD 21093 or call 410-560-2246.

Mary M. Jelinek has been an R.N. for many years. She carries a donor card and speaks out about this great gift. Little did she think that her first personal experience with organ donation would come through her own precious 39-year-old daughter.

Krista Lyn Johnson received her bachelor of arts, with high honors, and master of education from the University of Florida in 1993. She teaches kindergarten in South Florida. Krista enjoys traveling, skiing, swimming, rafting and working with children. She plans to write inspirational children's books.

Paul Karrer has published over 40 short stories and articles. He has taught kindergarten through college in Korea, England, American Samoa, Western Samoa, Connecticut and California. Currently, he is a fourth- and fifth-grade teacher in Castroville, California. He may be reached at 457 Archer St., Monterey, CA 93940 or call 408-655-9877.

Tim Kimmel is president of Generation Ministries, and he speaks on family issues throughout the United States and Canada. A graduate of Bryan College and Dallas Theological Seminary, Tim is also the author of *Homegrown Heroes* and *Raising Kids Who Turn Out Right.*

Mary Korzan was born in Elyria, Ohio and graduated from Bowling Green State University with a dual major in Early Childhood and Elementary Education. After working in the field of education for five years, she embraced her new role of motherhood. Currently, she is a stay-at-home mom with three children, Jennifer, Andrea and Joshua. She resides with her husband, Lee, at 17888 Buckland Dr., Granger, IN 46530.

Ted Kruger is a veteran of World War II and made four invasions into North Africa, Sicily, Italy and Utah Beach. He was given the name Israel Kurchetier and changed it legally to Ted Kruger in 1945. Ted retired in 1982, and now at the present age of 77, he has become a freelance writer. This is his first published material.

Lih Yuh Kuo is a renowned fashion designer in New York and a devoted mother of three. She received the 1996 Asian American Business Achievement Award for starting her company and label LIHLI which produces beautiful knit suits and dresses. She can be reached at 36 East 57th Street, New York, NY 10022 or call 718-937-5011.

Karrey Janvrin Lindenberg is a special education teacher in the Fort Dodge, Iowa Community School system. She is the mother of two sons, Andrew and Michael. She is a member of the Presbyterian church. Karrey is a graduate of the University of Iowa with an M.A. from Morningside College, Sioux City, Iowa. Karrey can be reached at 825 Forest Ave., Fort Dodge, IA 50501.

Patricia Lorenz, a frequent contributor to the *Chicken Soup* books, is an "art of living" inspirational writer, columnist and speaker. Over 400 of her articles have appeared in 75 publications, including *Reader's Digest, Guideposts, Woman's World, Working Mother* and *Single-Parent Family.* She is the author of two books, *Stuff That Matters for Single Parents* and *A Hug a Day for Single Parents,* published by Servant Publications in Ann Arbor, Michigan. You can write her at 7457 S. Pennsylvania Ave., Oak Creek, WI 53154.

Harvey Mackay is the author of *New York Times* #1 bestsellers, *Swim with the Sharks Without Being Eaten Alive* and *Beware the Naked Man Who Offers You His Shirt.* These books have been translated into 35 languages and distributed in 80 countries. His most recent book, *Sharkproof* also was a national bestseller. Harvey is a nationally syndicated columnist for United Features Syndicate, whose weekly articles appear in 50 newspapers around the country. He also is one of America's most popular and entertaining business speakers, speaking once a week to Fortune 500 companies and associations. Harvey is chairman and CEO of Mackay Envelope Corporation, a $60 million company he founded at age 26. He also is a partner in CogniTech Corp., an Atlanta-based software company that markets the contact management system, Sharkware.

Curt McAllister is a public-relations specialist based in Detroit, Michigan. He is also a former award-winning journalist and feature writer.

Karen Nordling McCowan has been a columnist for *The Register-Gard* in Eugene, Oregon since 1993. Before returning to her home state, she worked as a columnist, feature writer and reporter for *The Arizona Republic* in Phoenix. She has been married to Joel McCowan, a high school mathematics teacher, for 22 years. They have two daughters, Kelsey, 17 and Keeley, 12.

Mark Medoff is a dramatist and playright. He wrote many scripts for the show *Thirty Something* and wrote the book and the screenplay for *Children of a Lesser God, The Homage That Follows* (about to be released as a movie, *Homage*), *Red Ryder, Stumps, Stephanie Hero* and lots of other plays. He lives in New Mexico. He went to high school in Miami Beach. His work is being produced all over the U.S. in regional theaters.

Robert Tate Miller is an internationally published writer who has also worked as a television promotions writer/producer. He has written four screenplays and a number of essays on his early years growing up in a small North Carolina mountain town. He can be reached at 950 Hilgard Ave., Los Angeles, CA 90024.

Nancy Mitchell is the Director of Publishing for the Canfield Group. She handles the rights and permissions for all of the *Chicken Soup* projects. She and her sister, Patty, are co-authors with Jack and Mark of *Chicken Soup for the Surviving Soul*. Nancy can be reached by writing P.O. Box 30880, Santa Barbara, CA 93130 or call 800-237-8336.

Chick Moorman is the director of the Institute for Personal Power, a consulting firm dedicated to providing high-quality professional development activities for educators and parents. Every year he crisscrosses the country conducting over 100 workshops on cooperative learning, enhancing self-esteem and teaching respect and responsibility. His mission is to help people experience a greater sense of personal power in their love lives so they can in turn empower others. His latest book, *Where the Heart Is: Stories of Home and Family*, celebrates family strength, love, tolerance, hope and commitment. It can be ordered at $14.95 from Personal Power Press, P.O. Box 5985, Saginaw, MI 48603 or call 800-797-4133.

Janis A. Nark is a nurse, Vietnam veteran, entrepreneur and speaker. Surviving and excelling in six different professions on three different continents and through two wars, Janis knows about stress and change. Finding control in the chaos is her specialty; bringing humor, insight and awareness to others is her passion. You can contact Janis at 704-879-8080 or e-mail: JanisNark@aol.com.

Anne Newell is a retired detective from the Anchorage Police Department. She had created public safety radio programs and spoken in many arenas on safety, motivation and public speaking. She is an active member of Zonta International, International Training in Communication, HOBY, Anchorage Literacy Project and many community-based volunteer projects. You can contact Anne at 907-337-7268 or e-mail: anewell@aonline.com.

Varda One is a self-explorer who translates her discoveries into essays, poems, short stories, novels, songs and pamphlets, many of which have been published world-wide. Her hobby is reinventing herself by doing the impossible; her values are growth, enjoyment and youthfulness; her goal is to live to be a healthy, happy 101. She may be reached at 4218 A West 136th St., Hawthorne, CA 90250 or call 310-978-0799.

Thomas Overton is the compliance manager for the Information Technologies business unit at US West and president of a small real-estate development company. He has given talks to universities on paradigm shifts and related topics. As a community leader he is involved in many organizations and community activities including president of his optimist service club. Tom along with his wife of 31 years reside in Denver, CO. His greatest joy is his four children who are making their own positive mark on society.

Petey Parker is a national speaker, trainer and author. Her most recent book, *Corporate Kitty Litter: Turning No Way Attitudes into Know-How Solutions*, addresses the problems in corporate America and provides solutions that allow even one person to make a difference. Petey's presentations cover communication, strategic planning, team building and motivation. Her clients include J.C. Penney, Texas Instruments, Chilton, GTE, McKinsey & Company, and many national associations. For further information, call 800-893-6601.

Sara Parker is a teacher and writer who is currently seeking a publisher for her children's picture book, while working on a children's novel. She hopes to give her optimism and rose-colored view of life to her readers. She can be reached at 614 Bonita Dr., Aptos, CA 95003.

Dave Pelzer proudly carried the ceremonial flame for the 1996 Olympic Torch Relay and was the only American to receive the Outstanding Young Person of the World Award in 1994. Dave travels throughout the nation inspiring others to live a full, rich productive life. Often dubbed the "Robin Williams with glasses," no one touches the heart and challenges the human spirit as Dave Pelzer. For more information, write P.O. Box 1385, Guerneville, CA 95446 or call 707-869-2877.

Jude Revoli is a free-lance writer who has been published in *D Magazine*, *The Dallas Morning News*, *Texas Visions* and other publications in the Dallas-Fort Worth area. Jude is preparing for printing a volume of poetry and is continuing work on several other projects. Her specialty is "true life" stories. For information, contact Jude at 4021 Samuell Blvd., #125, Mesquite, TX 75149, or call 972-329-7397.

Percy Ross is an internationally known philanthropist, syndicated columnist, author and TV/radio personality. As a self-made millionaire, he has devoted himself to giving money, counsel, encouragement and hope to people from all walks of life. His *Thanks A Million* newspaper column appears in over 650 publications. Mr. Ross has publicly stated that he intends to give away his entire fortune during his lifetime, and his motto is, "He who gives while he lives . . . also knows where it goes."

Debbie Ross-Preston is a pharmaceutical sales rep in the Seattle area, specializing in public speaking to the plastic surgery and dermatology communities. She has been working toward her first marathon since finishing three half-marathons while she and her husband, Kent, are in the process of starting their family.

Russell L. (Rusty) Schweickart is President and CEO of ALOHA Networks, Inc. (ANI), a telecommunications technology company specializing in high-performance, wide-band multiple-access communications. Schweickart was formerly the Executive Vice President of CTA Commercial Systems, Inc. and Director of Low Earth Orbit (LEO) Systems. Schweickart's satellite and telecommunications work has involved him in the development of international communications regulations and policies.

Bonnie Shepherd, M.A., is an associate editor of *Focus on the Family* magazine. She is author of *Gestures of Love* and *A Bridge Called Compassion,* two collections of short stories about ordinary people doing extraordinary things. She earned her masters degree from the University of Illinois, Springfield and lives in Monument, CO. You may contact Bonnie at P.O. Box 1713, Monument, CO 80132 or call 719-488-1059.

Dr. Sidney B. Simon has been a teacher for 40 years and is a professor emeritus, psychological education, University of Massachusetts. He was a pioneer in values clarification, has written 14 books and is internationally known for his seminars and workshops. An award winner for his presentations, he is in high demand for keynotes and workshops, when he isn't bicycling the world, canoeing the seas and computing the Internet. You may contact Sidney at 45 Old Mountain Rd., Hadley, MA 01035 or call 413-584-4382.

Bill Simpson is a United Methodist pastor, writer and speaker. The author of three books and numerous articles, Dr. Simpson serves as one of the editors of *The Living Pulpit* magazine. He is known for his work in Huguenot church history. He is currently senior pastor of Front Street United Methodist Church, Burlington, NC and can be reached through Box 2597, Burlington, NC 27216 or call 910-227-6263; e-mail: fsumc@netpath.net.

Joanna Slan is a full-time professional speaker and author and believes the life we live is the life we create. A top-ranked presenter, Joanna speaks all across the country and the globe on gender issues. An award-winning communicator, her work has appeared in newspapers, magazines and on television. She is the author of four books including *I'm Too Blessed to Be Depressed.* Joanna has hosted a television talk show, studied under Dr. W. Edwards Deming and written speeches for multinational executives for Chrysler-Mitsubishi. Joanna lives in St. Louis, Missouri, with her husband David and son, Michael.

Shari Smith, a former middle-school math teacher in Texas and Florida, is currently the Income Development Director for the American Cancer Society in Austin, Texas. Her motivation for teaching and helping others is derived from her loving family, the many students that taught her valuable lessons and her relationship with Christ. Like "Thelma," Shari is optimistic about the future.

Martha Pendergrass Templeton enjoys writing, storytelling and teaching eighth grade at Summerville Middle School. She is the director of "Kids for Christ," a troupe that incorporates clowning, puppeteering and storytelling in ministry to children. She can be reached at 83 Rd. 932, Mentone, AL 35984.

Diane Brucato Thomas, founder of "Hawaii Institute for Wellness in Dentistry," is a "gum gardner" who "digs" what she does. Diane also has a gift for storytelling. Her performances for gatherings of all ages have enriched many lives. Diane and her family live at a place she calls "The Cafe at the Edge of the World." She can be reached at P.O. Box 2065, Pahoa, HI 96778.

Dolly Trout is a San Joaquin Valley resident who has taught in Fresno County schools for 25 years. She earned her master's degree in special education at California State University, San Francisco. As a fifth-year mentor teacher, she is an enthusiastic and dedicated speaker, giving personal growth seminars and experiential workshops on self-actualization. Dolly became a trainer in values clarification at the University of San Diego under the expert guidance of Dr. Sidney and Suzanne Simon. She authored the book *Toward Building a Better Future . . . A Guide to Adult Service Providers in Fresno County*.

Michele Vignola spent four years as a political activist, coordinator and para-legal for the Leonard Peltier Defense Committee. Her experiences include public speaking, radio and television. Currently she resides in Lawrence, Kansas as a teacher of drama. She also enjoys writing as a hobby.

Judy Walker was born in Birmingham, Alabama, and has three sons, one daughter and one stepson. She has worked for the Social Security Administration for 15 years, and is currently an SSI Claims Representative in the Oklahoma City office. Judy and her late husband, Robert, who died in the Oklahoma City bombing, transferred to Oklahoma City from Albuquerque, NM in 1992.

Ann E. Weeks has had a private practice as a nurse family therapist for 21 years. She works with individuals, couples and families dealing with life's passages and stresses. In her years of practice she has developed a variety of strategies to facilitate healing and learning. Humor is one of the truly effective ones to "help the medicine go down." Dr. Weeks is a member of the National Speakers Association and the American Association for Therapeutic Humor. She is a nationally known speaker who gives her audiences many everyday strategies to heal the stresses of life's passages.

Sharon Whitley, a former special education teacher, is the recipient of several writing awards, including the *Atlantic Monthly*. Her work has appeared in *Reader's Digest* (including 18 international editions), *Los Angeles Times Magazine, Guideposts* and *New Woman*. She can be reached at 5666 Meredith Avenue, San Diego, CA 92120 or call 619-583-7346.

Bettie B. Youngs, Ph.D., Ed.D., is an international lecturer and consultant living in Del Mar, California. She is the author of 14 books published in 28 languages including the bestseller *Values from the Heartland*. Her story is reprinted from *Gifts of the Heart* (Health Communications, Inc.). You can contact Bettie by writing to 3060 Racetrack View Dr., Del Mar, CA 92014.

Permissions

We would like to acknowledge the following publishers and individuals for permission to reprint the following material. (Note: The stories that were penned anonymously, that are public domain, or that were written by Jack Canfield, Mark Victor Hansen, Hanoch McCarty or Meladee McCarty are not included in this listing.)

A Friend on the Line. Reprinted by permission of Jennings Michael Burch. ©1966 Jennings Michael Burch.

Simple Wooden Boxes. Reprinted with permission from Martha Pendergrass Templeton. ©1995 by Martha Pendergrass Templeton.

A Family for Freddie. Reprinted with permission from December 1964 *Reader's Digest.* Copyright ©1964 by The Reader's Digest Assn., Inc.

A Birthday Song, Cookies Forgotten and Forgiven, Calling on a Girl Named Becky and *A Tale of Canine Courage.* Reprinted with permission from *Reader's Digest* and *The Christian Science Monitor* ©1994 Robert Tate Miller.

When Kevin Won. Reprinted by permission of Janice M. Gibson. ©1996 Janice M. Gibson.

Beautiful on the Inside. Reprinted by permission of Pamela J. deRoy. ©1996 Pamela J. deRoy.

Such As I Have. Reprinted by permission of Bonnie Shepherd. ©1996 Bonnie Shepherd.

A Hair-Raising Experience. Reprinted by permission of Debbie Ross-Preston. ©1996 Debbie Ross-Preston.

Money of My Own. Reprinted with permission by publisher Health Communications, Inc., Deerfield Beach, Florida, from *Gifts of the Heart* by Bettie B. Youngs, ©1996 Bettie B. Youngs.

Hi, Cornelius. Reprinted by permission of Bob Greene. Excerpted from *Hang Time: Days and Dreams with Michael Jordan.* ©1992 Bob Greene.

Changed Lives. Excerpted from the book *Tender Warrior* by Stu Weber; Multnomah Books, Questor Publishers; ©1993 by Stu Weber.

Directory Assistance. Reprinted by permission of Joanna Slan. ©1996 Joanna Slan.

Cold Hands. Reprinted by permission of Joyce Andresen. ©1996 Joyce Andresen.

The Woodwork Angel. Reprinted by permission of Varda One. ©1996 Varda One.

The 11th Box. Reprinted by permission of Pastor Bill Simpson. ©1994 Bill Simpson.

Don't Pass Me By. Reprinted by permission of Jude Revoli. ©1996 Jude Revoli.

Bidding from the Heart. Reprinted by permission of *The Columbus (Ohio) Dispatch.* ©1996 *The Columbus Dispatch.*

Ask for the Moon and Get It. Reprinted by permission of Percy Ross. ©1994 Percy Ross.

Passing on Small Change. Reprinted by permission of Nancy Mitchell. ©1996 Nancy Mitchell.

Big Feet—Bigger Heart and *Encouragement.* Reprinted from *The Sower's Seeds* by permission of Paulist Press. ©1994 Brian Cavanaugh.

Improving Your Life Every Day

Real people sharing real stories — for nineteen years. Now, Chicken Soup for the Soul has gone beyond the bookstore to become a world leader in life improvement. Through books, movies, DVDs, online resources and other partnerships, we bring hope, courage, inspiration and love to hundreds of millions of people around the world. Chicken Soup for the Soul's writers and readers belong to a one-of-a-kind global community, sharing advice, support, guidance, comfort, and knowledge.

Chicken Soup for the Soul stories have been translated into more than 40 languages and can be found in more than one hundred countries. Every day, millions of people experience a Chicken Soup for the Soul story in a book, magazine, newspaper or online. As we share our life experiences through these stories, we offer hope, comfort and inspiration to one another. The stories travel from person to person, and from country to country, helping to improve lives everywhere.

Chicken Soup for the Soul.

Share with Us

We all have had Chicken Soup for the Soul moments in our lives. If you would like to share your story or poem with millions of people around the world, go to chickensoup.com and click on "Submit Your Story." You may be able to help another reader, and become a published author at the same time. Some of our past contributors have launched writing and speaking careers from the publication of their stories in our books!

Our submission volume has been increasing steadily — the quality and quantity of your submissions has been fabulous. We only accept story submissions via our website. They are no longer accepted via mail or fax.

To contact us regarding other matters, please send us an e-mail through webmaster@chickensoupforthesoul.com, or fax or write us at:

Chicken Soup for the Soul
P.O. Box 700
Cos Cob, CT 06807-0700
Fax: 203-861-7194

One more note from your friends at Chicken Soup for the Soul: Occasionally, we receive an unsolicited book manuscript from one of our readers, and we would like to respectfully inform you that we do not accept unsolicited manuscripts and we must discard the ones that appear.

Chicken Soup for the Soul®

The Power of Positive

101 Inspirational Stories about Changing Your Life through Positive Thinking

Jack Canfield,
Mark Victor Hansen,
and Amy Newmark

Attitude is everything. And this book will uplift and inspire readers with its 101 success stories about the power of positive thinking and how contributors changed their lives, solved problems, or overcame challenges through a positive attitude, counting their blessings, or other epiphanies.

978-1-61159-903-9

Chicken Soup
for the Soul.

Think
Positive

101 Inspirational
Stories about
Counting Your Blessings and
Having a Positive Attitude

Jack Canfield,
Mark Victor Hansen & Amy Newmark
Foreword by Deborah Norville

Every cloud has a silver lining. Readers will be inspired by these 101 real-life stories from people just like them, taking a positive attitude to the ups and downs of life, and remembering to be grateful and count their blessings. This book continues Chicken Soup for the Soul's focus on inspiration and hope, and its stories of optimism and faith will encourage readers to stay positive during challenging times and in their everyday lives.

978-1-935096-56-6

Chicken Soup for the Soul®

Count Your Blessings

101 Stories of Gratitude, Fortitude, and Silver Linings

Jack Canfield,
Mark Victor Hansen, Amy Newmark,
Laura Robinson & Elizabeth Bryan

This uplifting book reminds readers of the blessings in their lives, despite financial stress, natural disasters, health scares and illnesses, housing challenges and family worries. This feel-good book is a great gift for New Year's or Easter, for someone going through a difficult time, or for Christmas. These stories of optimism, faith, and strength remind us of the simple pleasures of family, home, health, and inexpensive good times.

978-1-935096-42-9

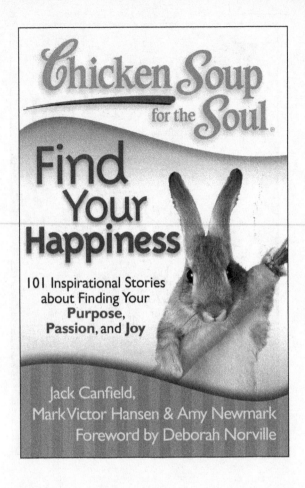

Chicken Soup for the Soul.

Find Your Happiness

101 Inspirational Stories about Finding Your **Purpose, Passion,** and **Joy**

Jack Canfield,
Mark Victor Hansen & Amy Newmark
Foreword by Deborah Norville

Others share how they found their passion, purpose, and joy in life in these 101 personal and exciting stories that are sure to encourage readers to find their own happiness. Stories in this collection will inspire readers to pursue their dreams, find their passion and seek joy in their life. This book continues Chicken Soup for the Soul's focus on inspiration and hope, reminding readers that they can find their own happiness.

978-1-935096-77-1

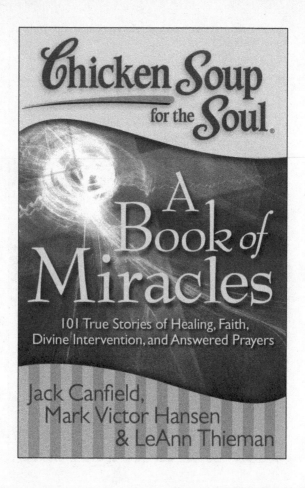

Chicken Soup for the Soul®

A Book of Miracles

101 True Stories of Healing, Faith, Divine Intervention, and Answered Prayers

Jack Canfield,
Mark Victor Hansen
& LeAnn Thieman

Everyone loves a good miracle story, and this book provides 101 true stories of healing, divine intervention, and answered prayers. These amazing, personal stories prove that God is alive and active in the world today, working miracles on our behalf. The incredible accounts show His love and involvement in our lives. This book of miracles will encourage, uplift, and recharge the faith of Catholics and all Christian readers.

978-1-935096-51-1

Chicken Soup for the Soul.

Inspirational Stories and Medical Advice for a Healthy You!

by DR. MARIE PASINSKI of HARVARD MEDICAL SCHOOL
with LIZ NEPORENT

Boost Your Brain Power!

You Can Improve and Energize Your Brain at Any Age

A great guide to powering up your brain...
and I loved the motivational stories too!
~ Dr. Joe Shrand

Inspiring Chicken Soup for the Soul stories and accessible leading-edge medical information from Dr. Marie Pasinski of Harvard Medical School. Many people would like to enhance their brainpower and are looking for help to do just that. Others are retraining their brains after traumatic injuries or strokes. Others are looking for ways to keep their brains young and dynamic. This book will fascinate you with stories and useful information on how to improve your own brain.

978-1-935096-86-3

Chicken Soup for the Soul.

Devotional Stories for Tough Times

101 Daily Devotions to Inspire and Support You in Times of Need

Susan M. Heim
and Karen C. Talcott
Foreword by Mary Beth Chapman

Struggles test us all, but readers will find counsel and reassurance in these devotional stories of faith, strength, and prayer. This collection is filled with stories that show God's presence during times of trouble—from illness, addictions, job loss, grief, and much more—providing a boost and reminder of God's ever-present love. Readers will find encouragement, solace, and hope in these personal stories and prayers.

978-1-935096-74-0

Dating and courtship, romance, love, and marriage are favorite Chicken Soup for the Soul topics. Everyone loves to read true stories about how it happened for other people. This book includes the 101 best stories on love and marriage that appeared in a wide variety of past Chicken Soup for the Soul books. These heartwarming stories will inspire and amuse readers, whether they are just starting to date, are newly wed, or are veterans of a long marriage.

978-1-935096-10-8

Chicken Soup for the Soul.

Inspiration for the Young at Heart

101 Stories of Inspiration, Humor, and Wisdom about Life at a Certain Age

Jack Canfield, Mark Victor Hansen, and Amy Newmark

Life begins again at 60! Crossing that magic age might bring a few new wrinkles but also new experiences, and this book celebrates all the fun and wonder of getting older. Readers will revel in these 101 new stories by other dynamic older singles and couples who are actively enjoying their "senior years!" Filled with humorous and fun adventures of love, family, travel, careers, and new pursuits, this book will delight and invigorate readers.

978-1-935096-71-9

Chicken Soup for the Soul

for the

My Resolution

101 Heartwarming,
Healthful, and
Humorous
Resolutions...

...and how they
turned out!

Jack Canfield,
Mark Victor Hansen,
D'ette Corona & Barbara LoMonaco

Everyone makes resolutions—for New Year's, for big birthdays, for new school years. In fact, most of us are so good at resolutions that we make the same ones year after year. This collection of great true stories covers topics such as losing weight, getting organized, stopping bad habits, restoring relationships, dealing with substance abuse, changing jobs, going green, and even today's hot topic—dealing with the economic crisis.

978-1-935096-28-3

www.chickensoup.com